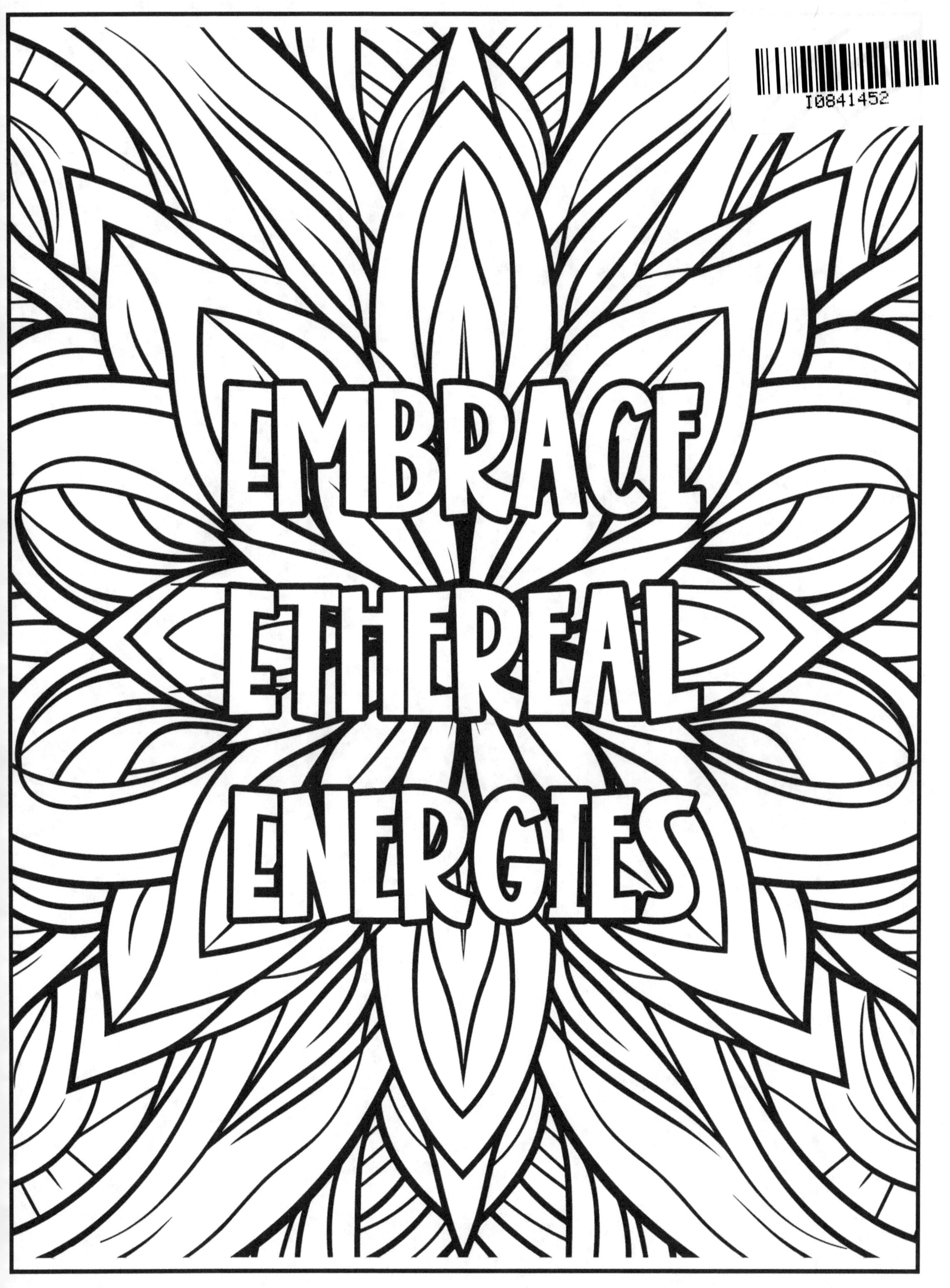

EMBRACE
ETHEREAL
ENERGIES

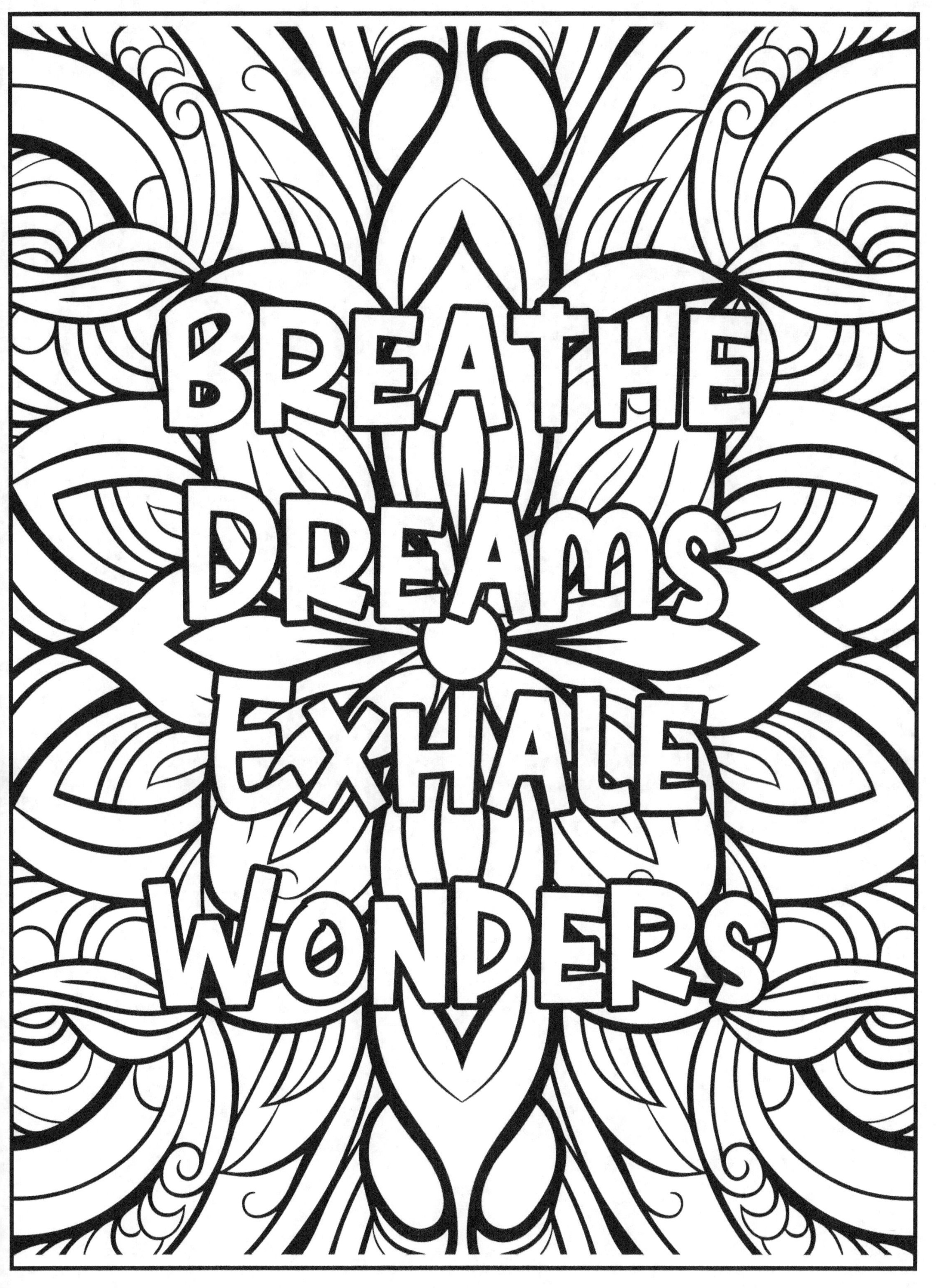

BREATHE
DREAMS
EXHALE
WONDERS

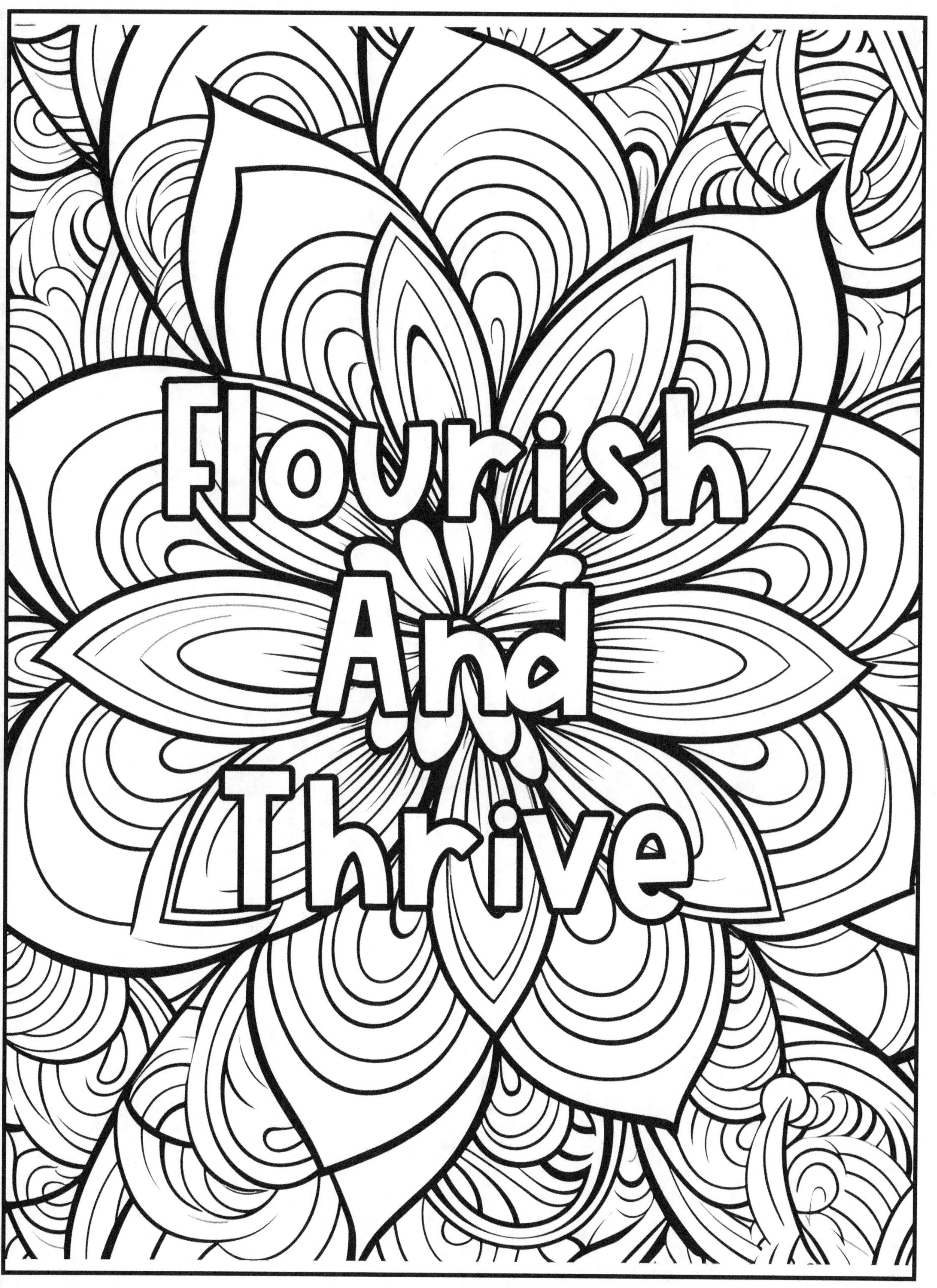

Flourish
And
Thrive

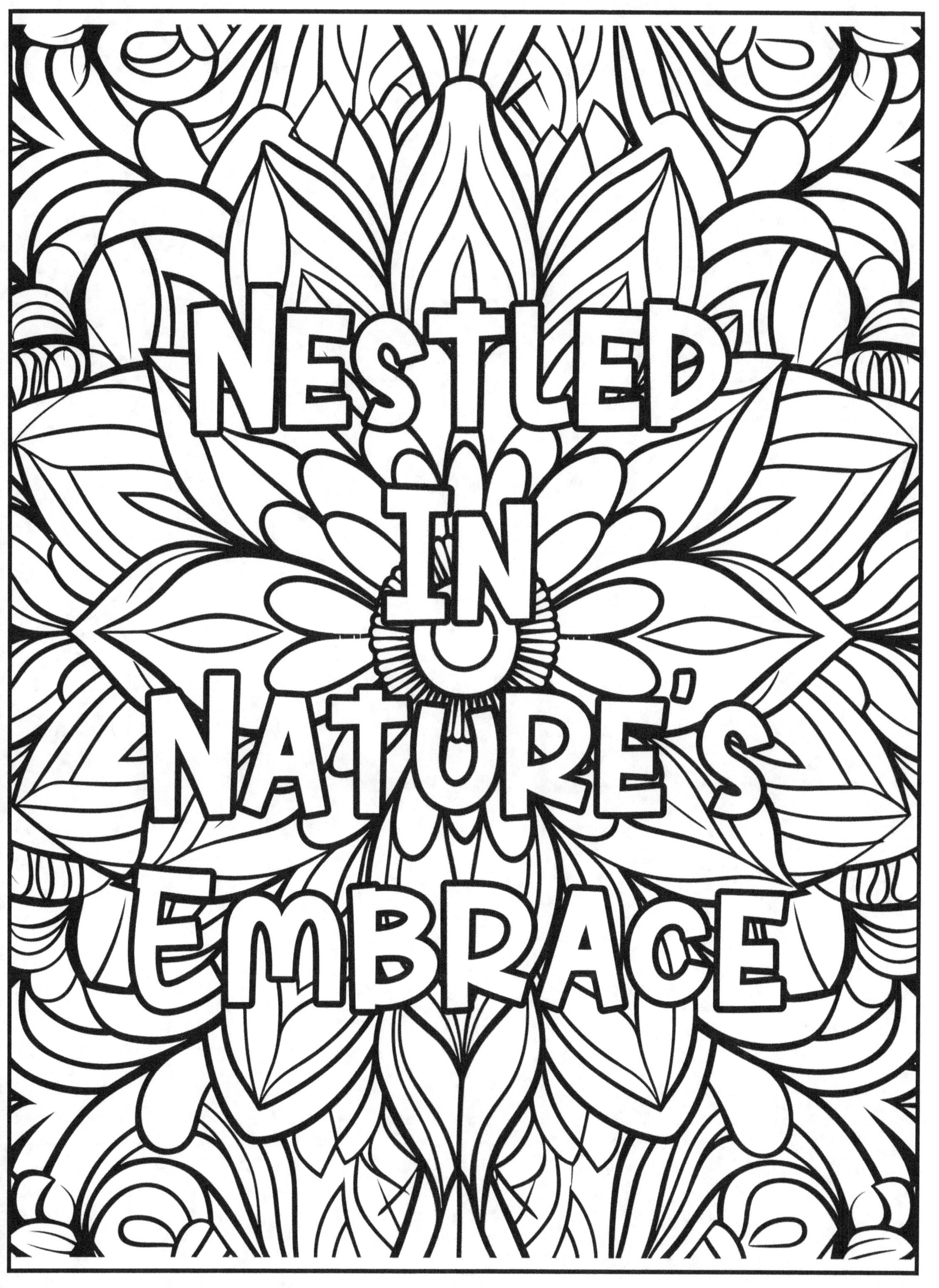

NESTLED
IN
NATURE'S
EMBRACE

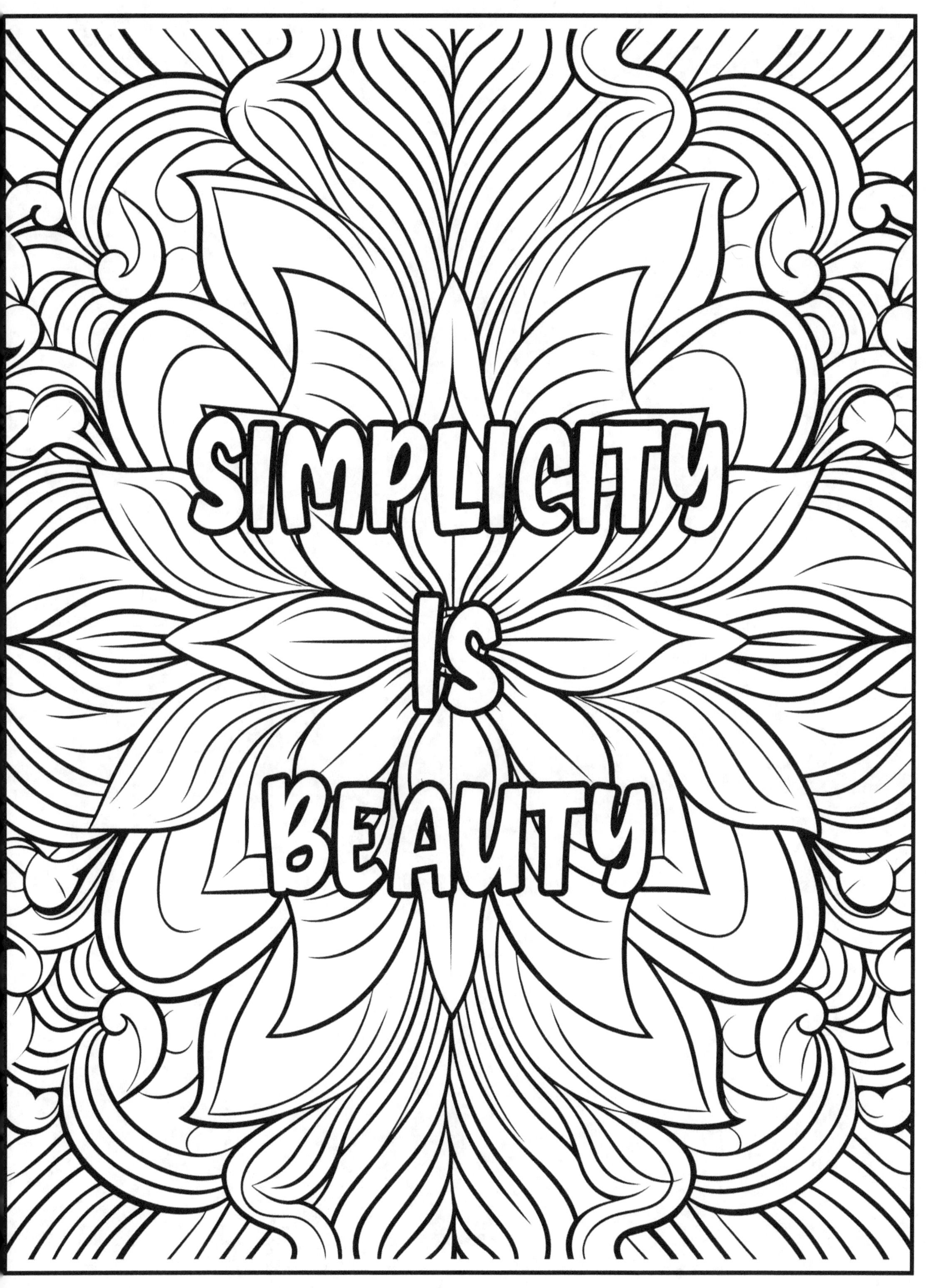

SIMPLICITY
IS
BEAUTY

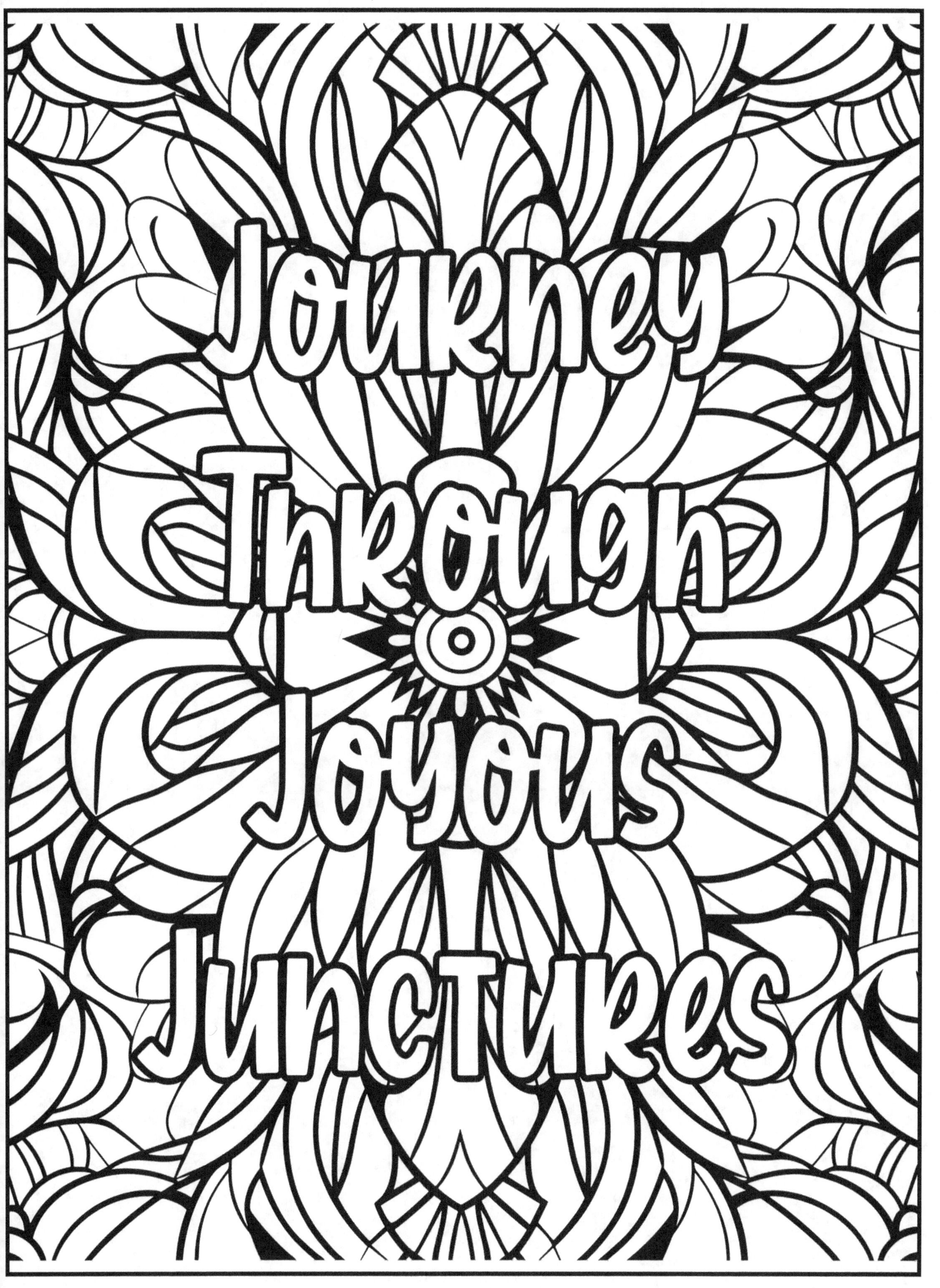

Journey
Through
Joyous
Junctures

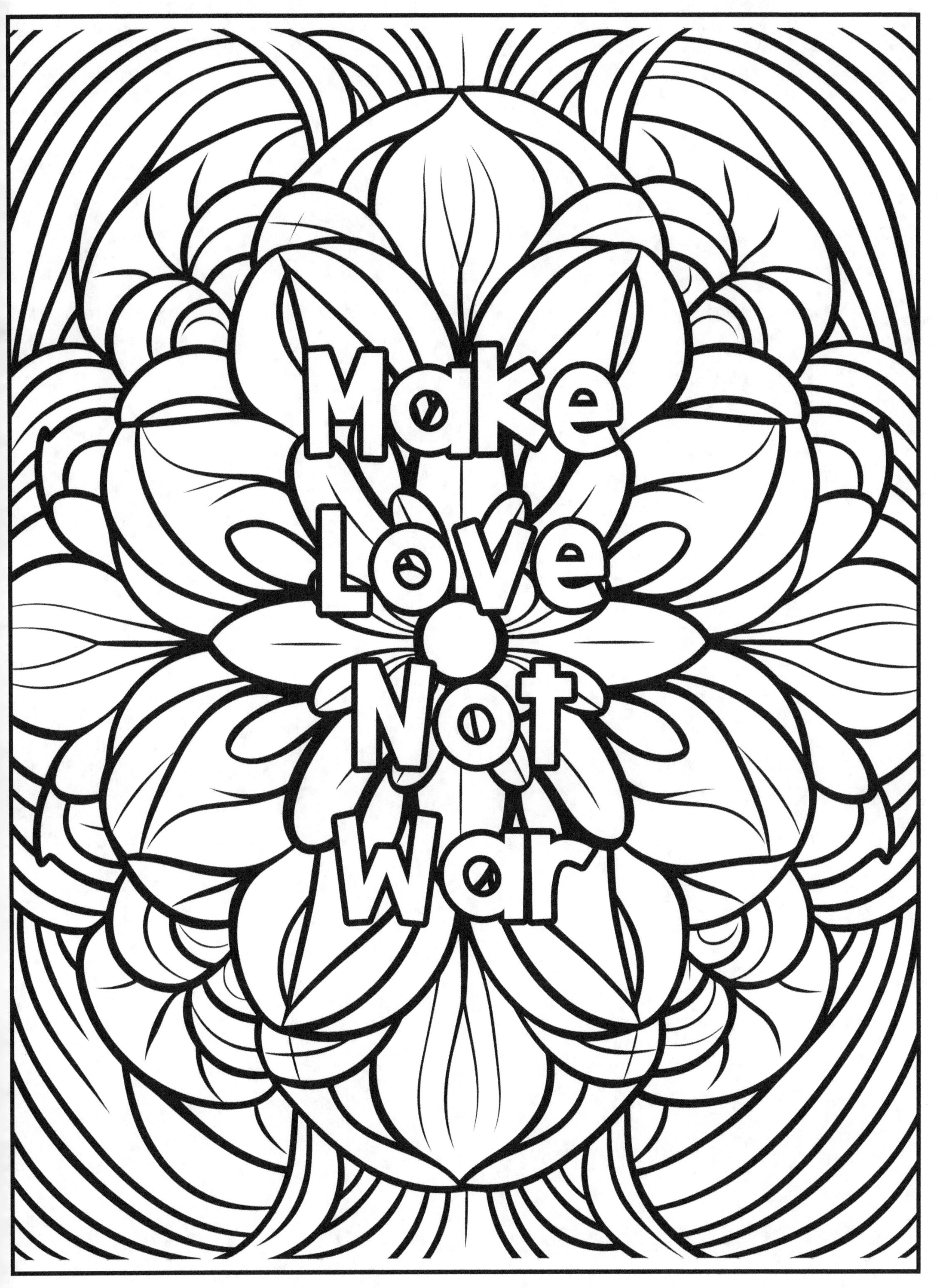

Make
Love
Not
War

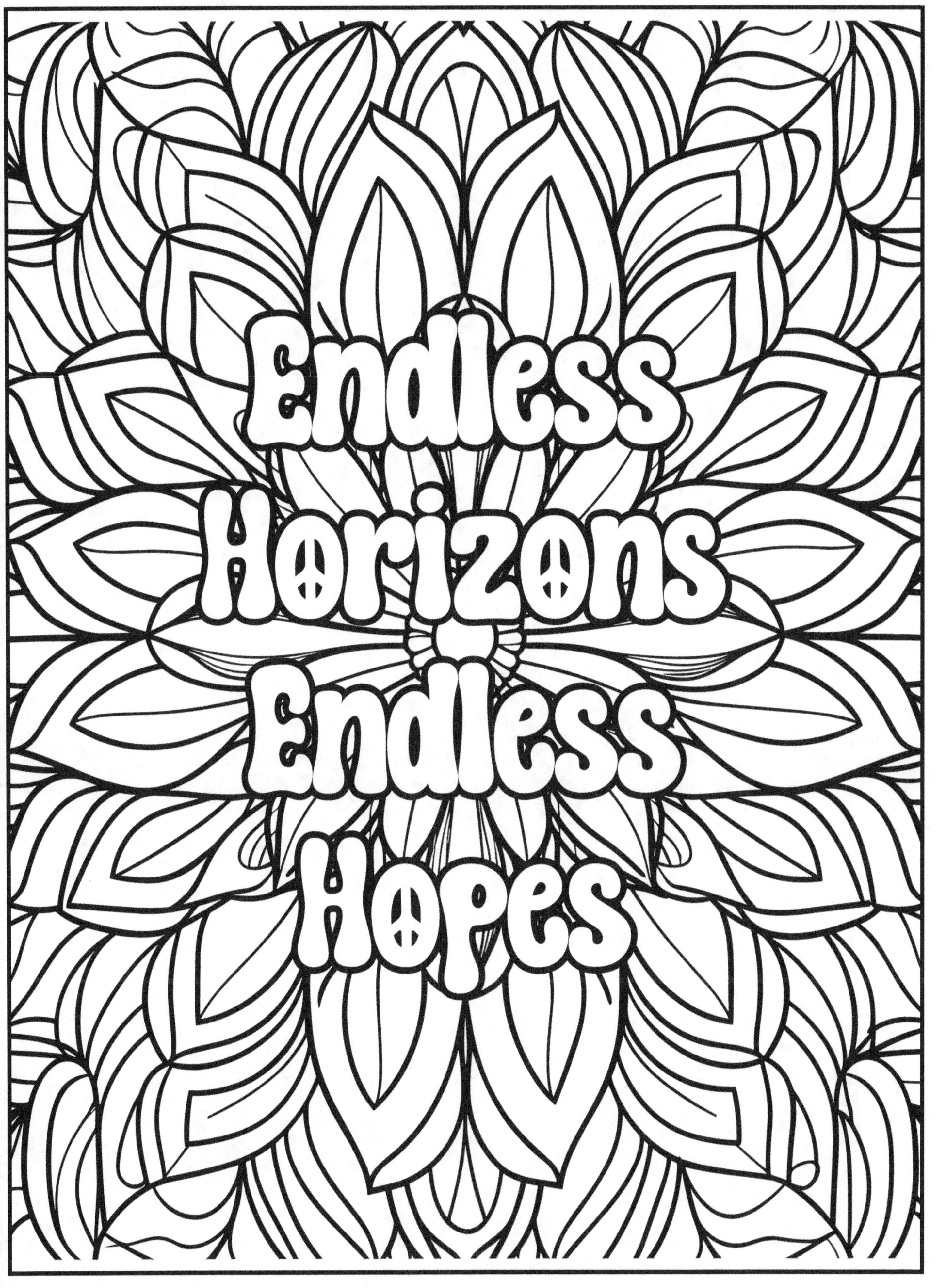

Endless
Horizons
Endless
Hopes

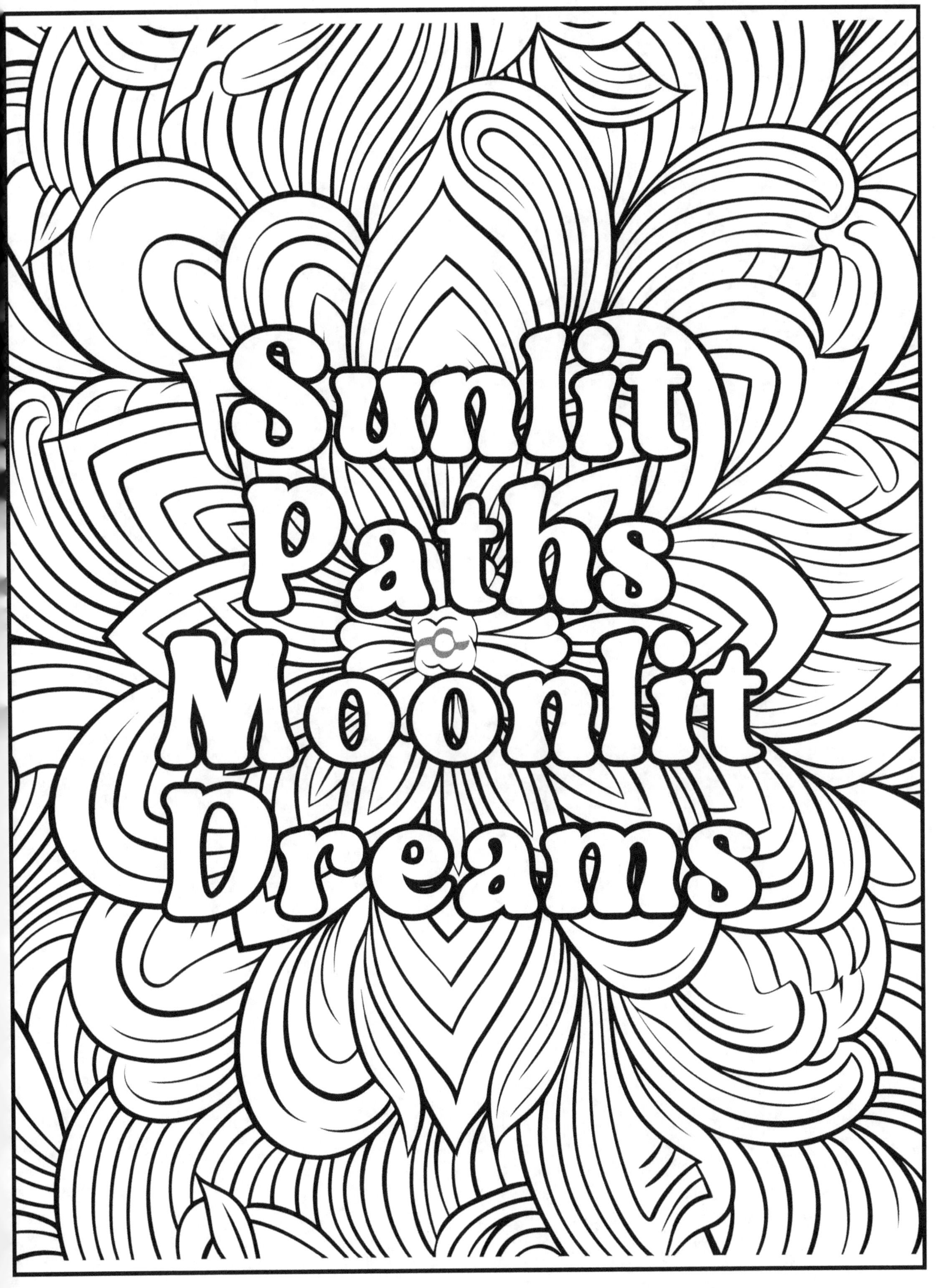
Sunlit
Paths
Moonlit
Dreams

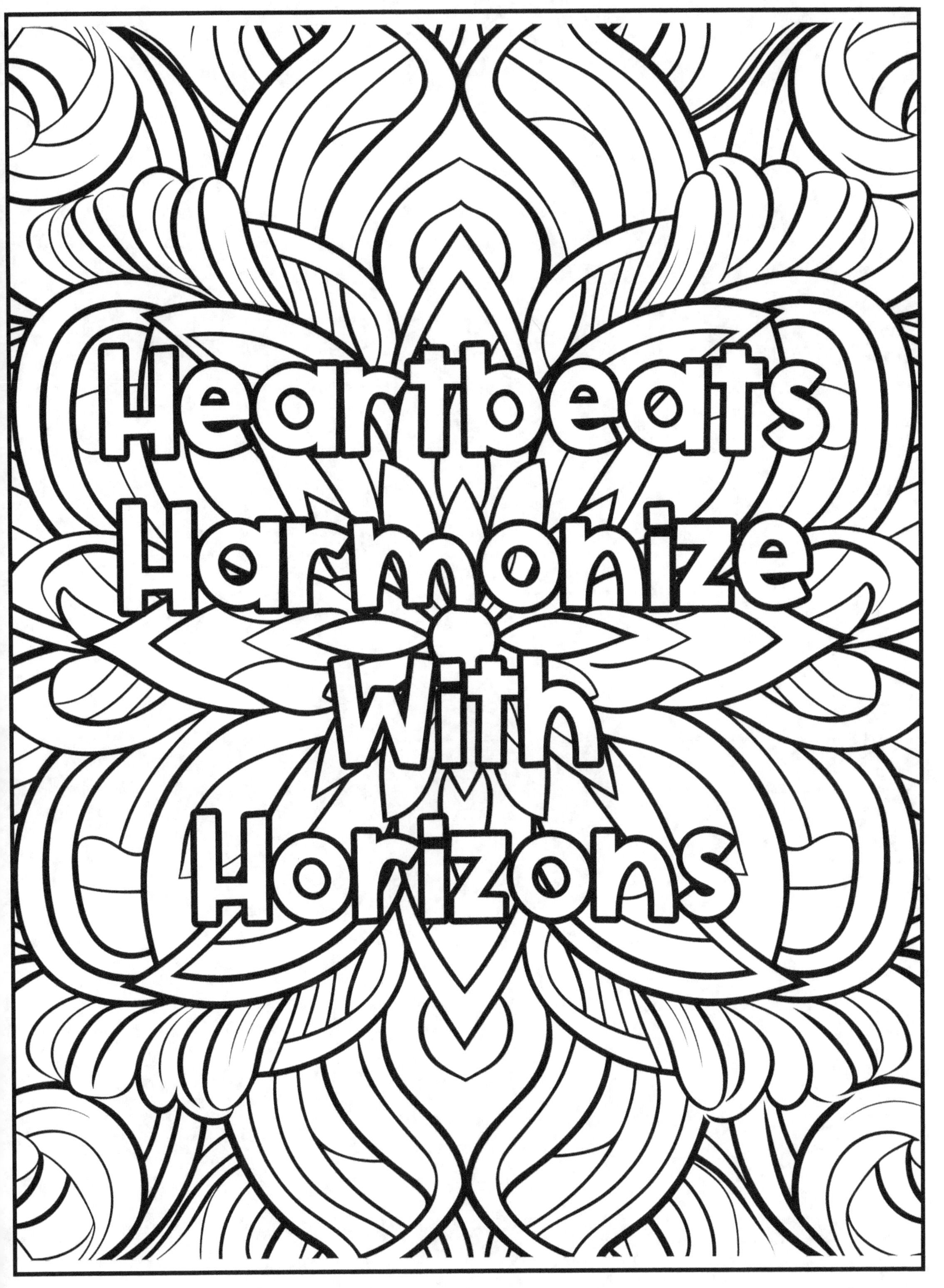

Heartbeats
Harmonize
With
Horizons

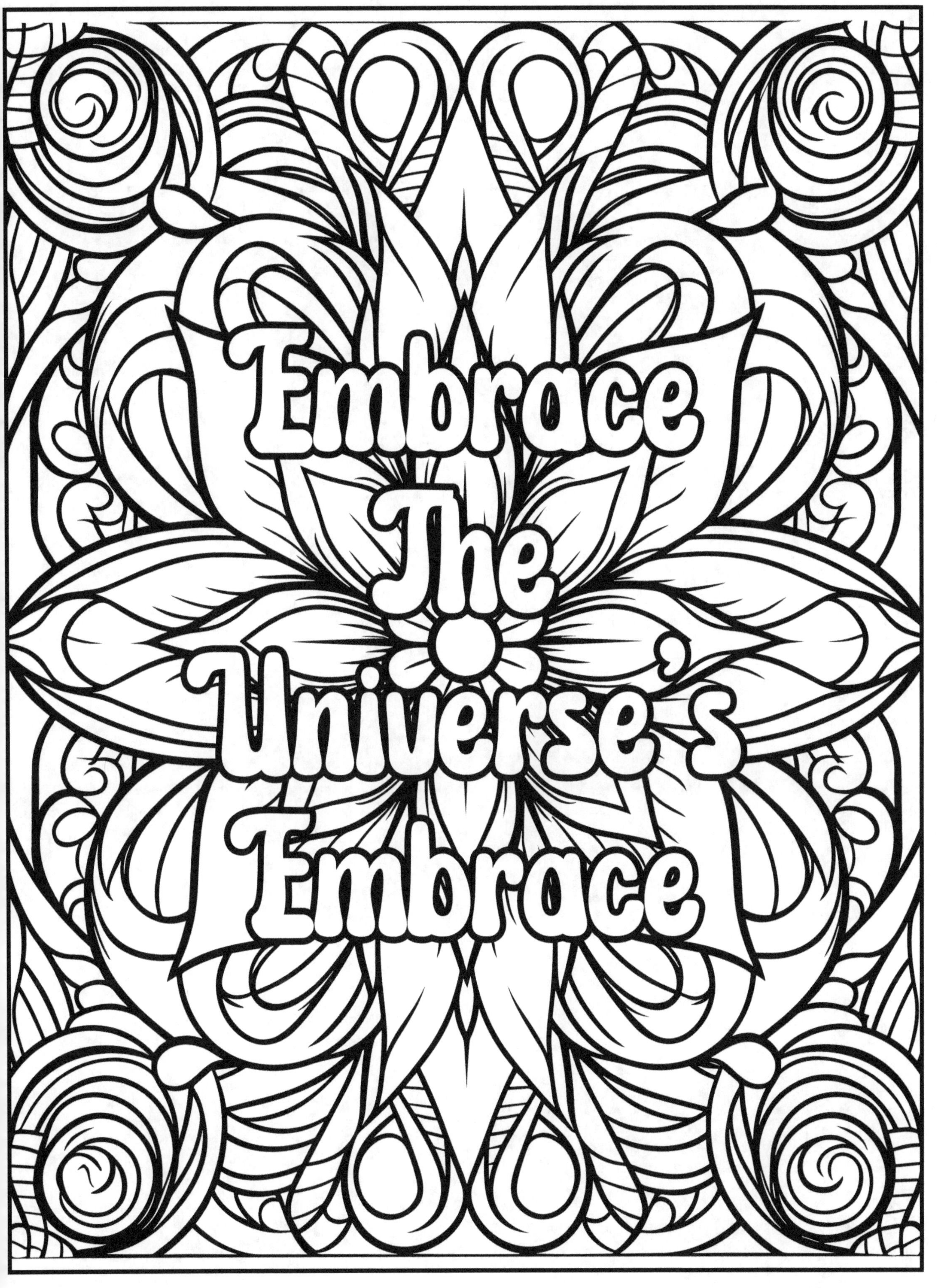

Embrace
The
Universe's
Embrace

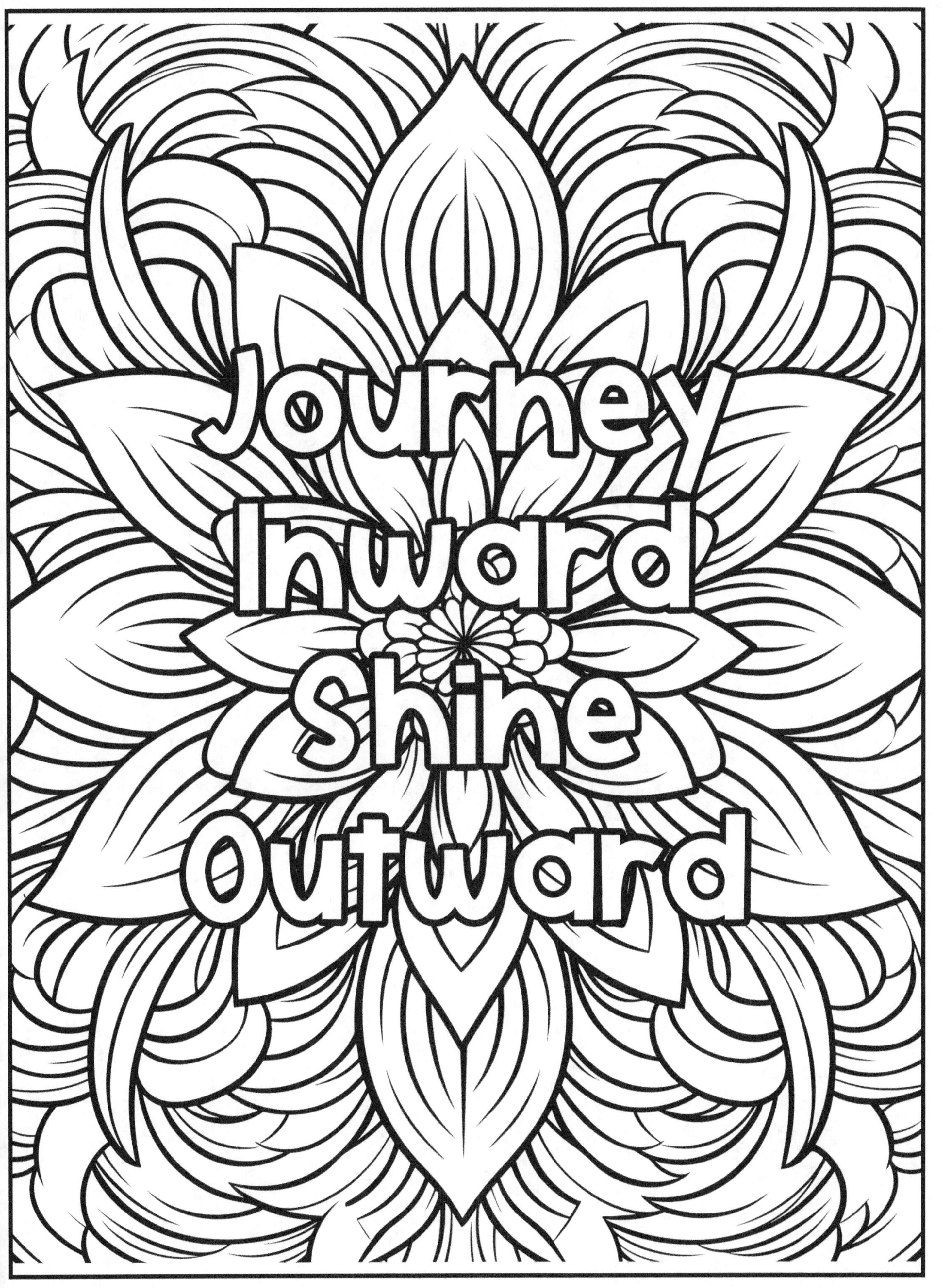

Journey
Inward
Shine
Outward

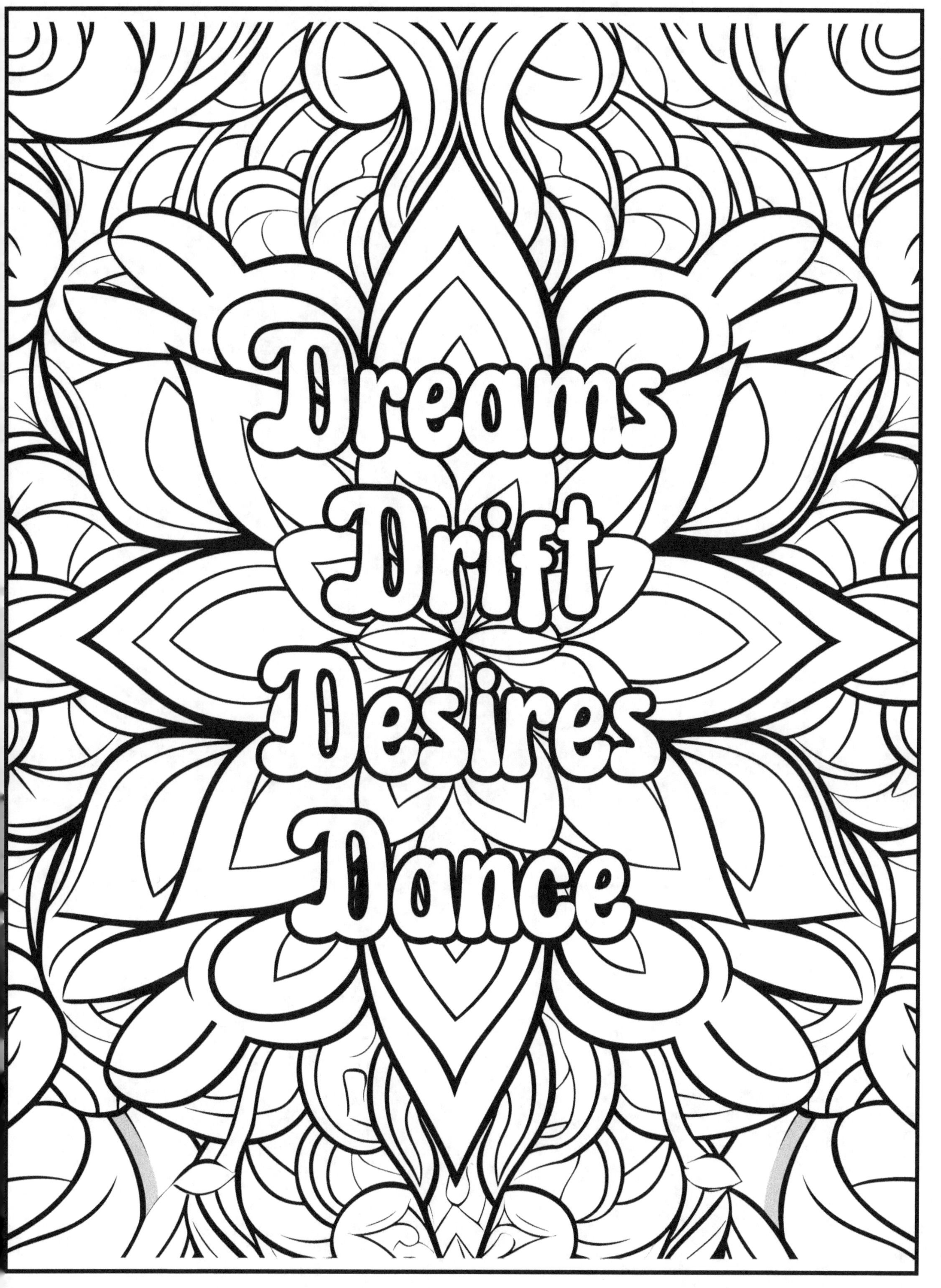

Dreams
Drift
Desires
Dance

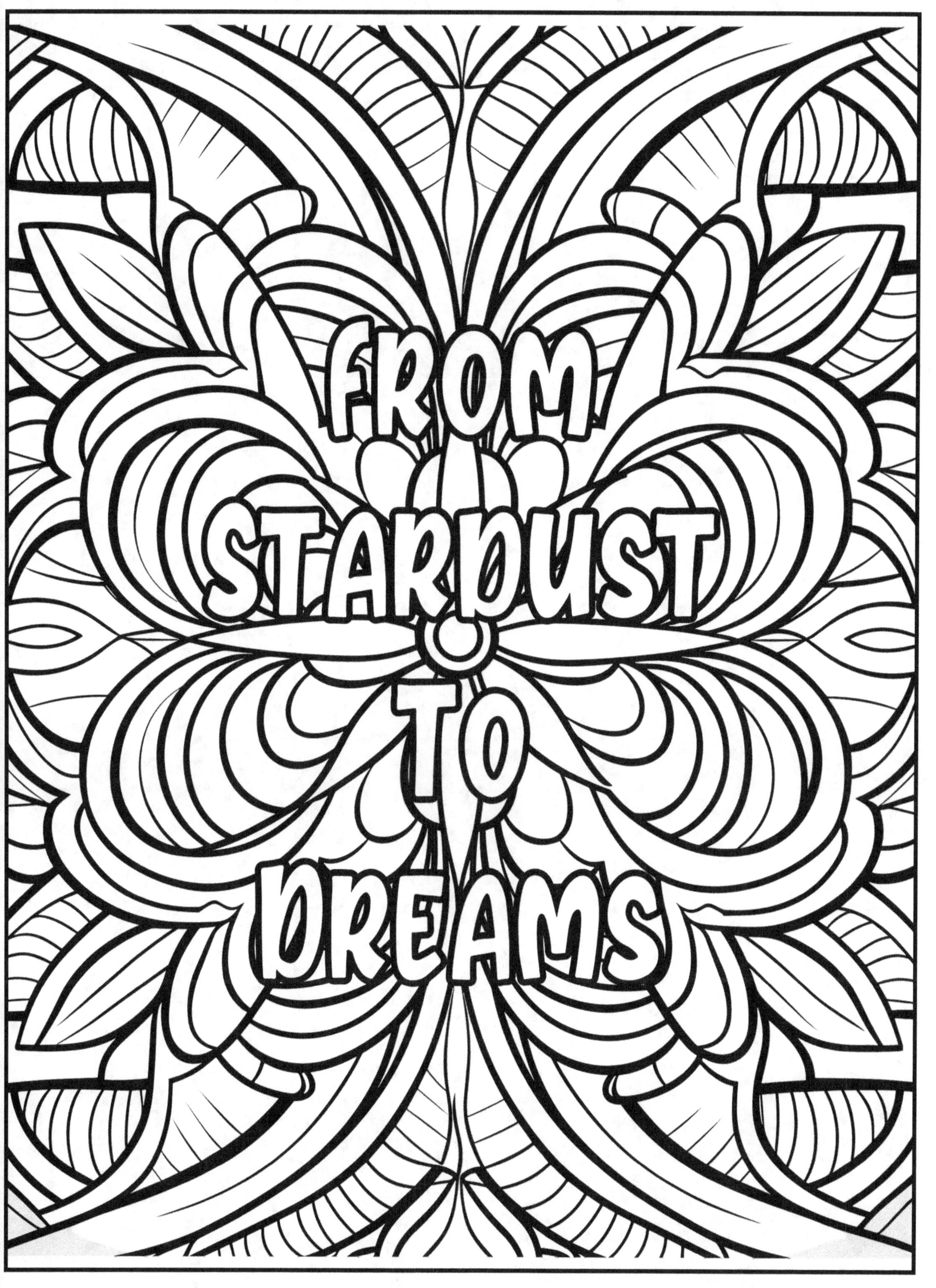

FROM
STARDUST
TO
DREAMS

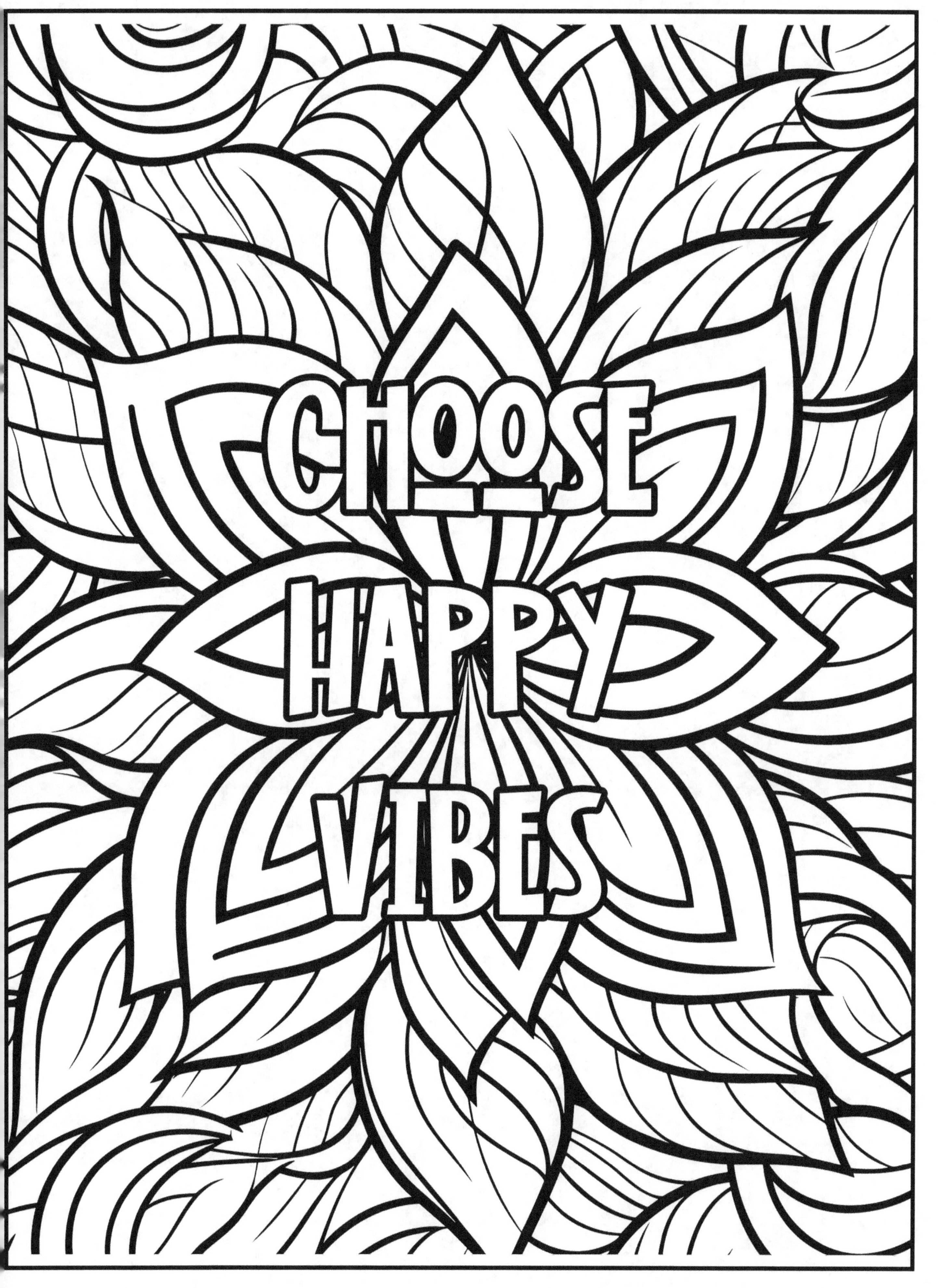

CHOOSE
HAPPY
VIBES

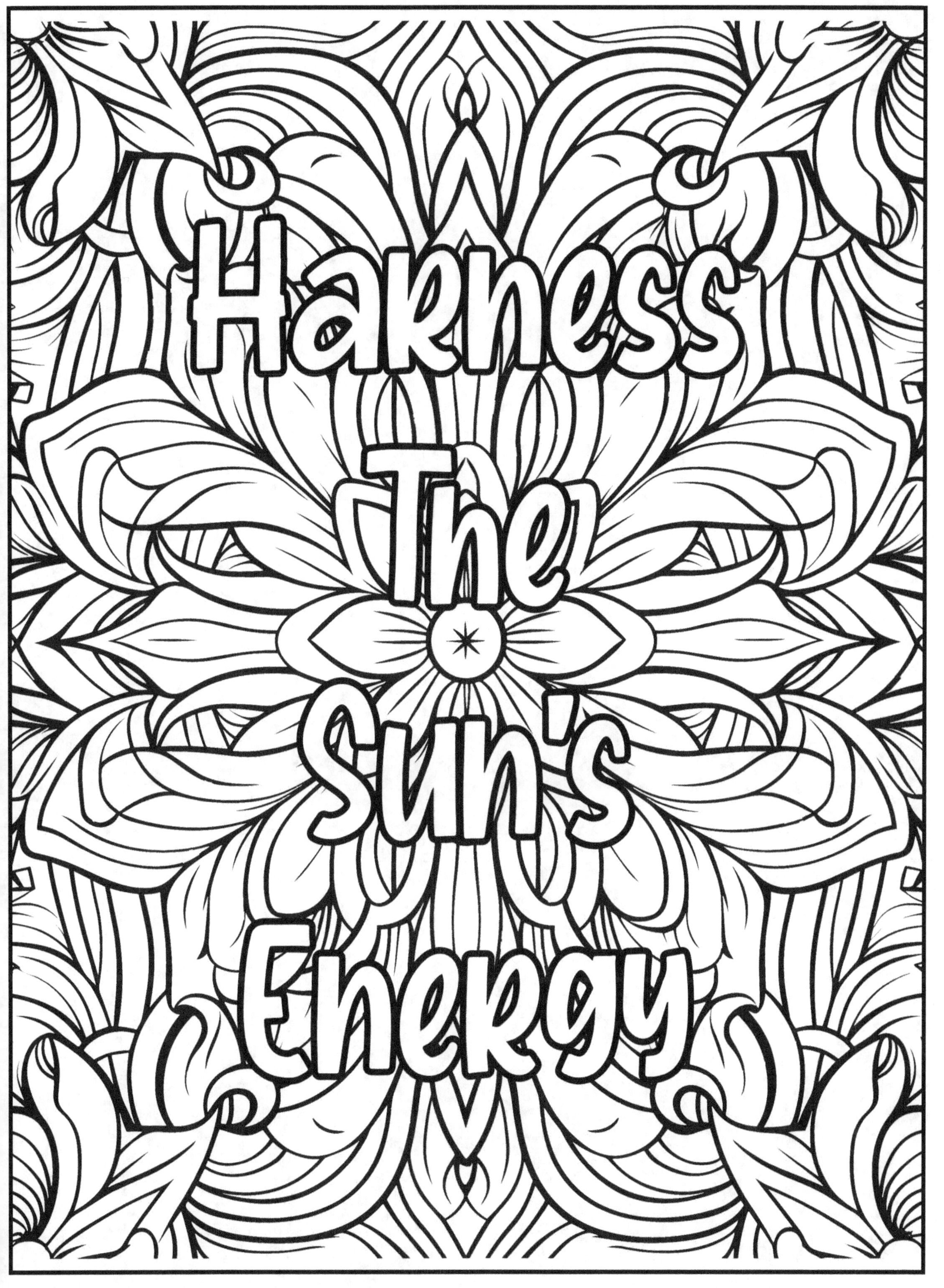

Harness
The
Sun's
Energy

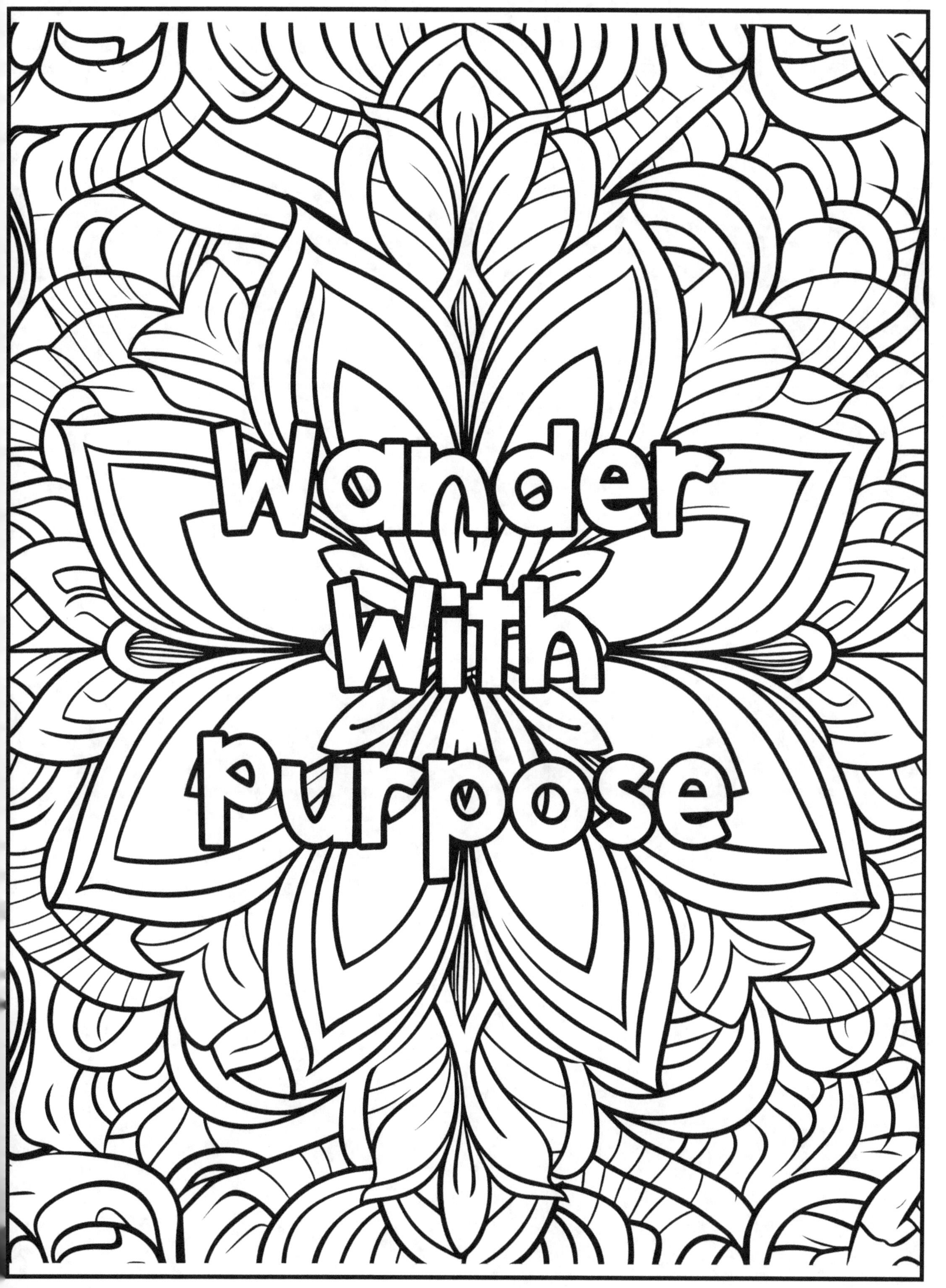

Wander
With
purpose

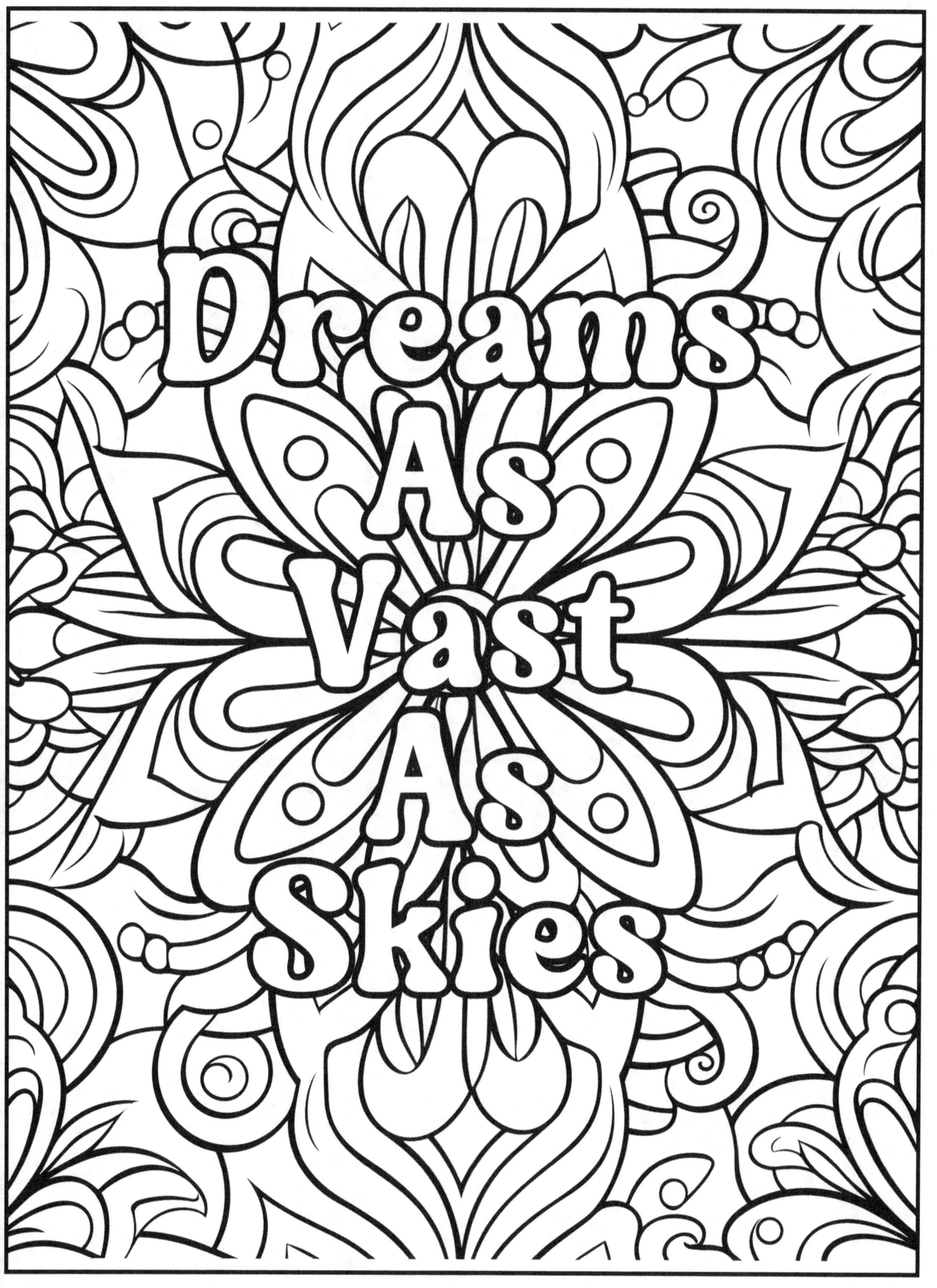

Dreams
As
Vast
As
Skies

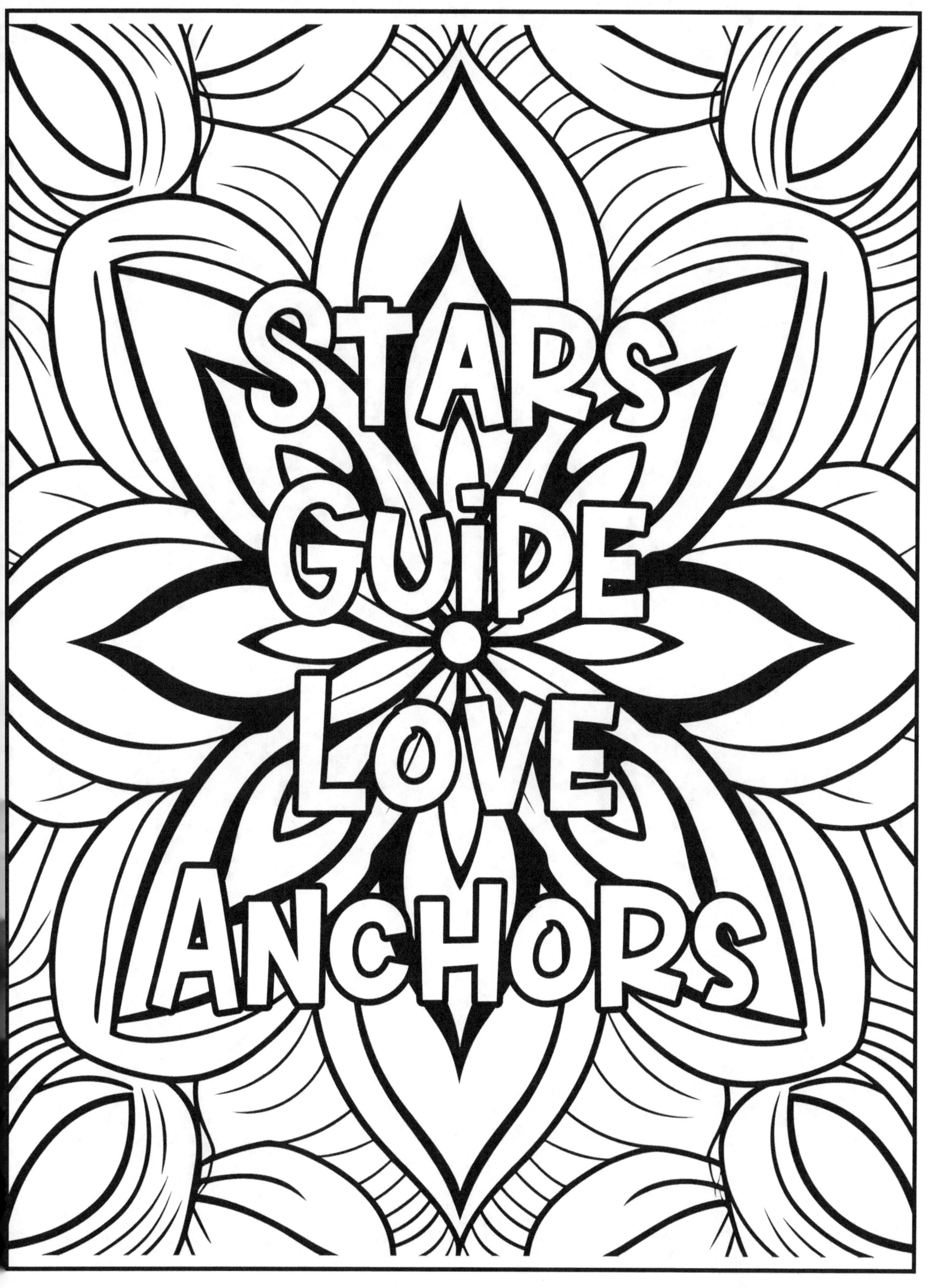

Stars
Guide
Love
Anchors

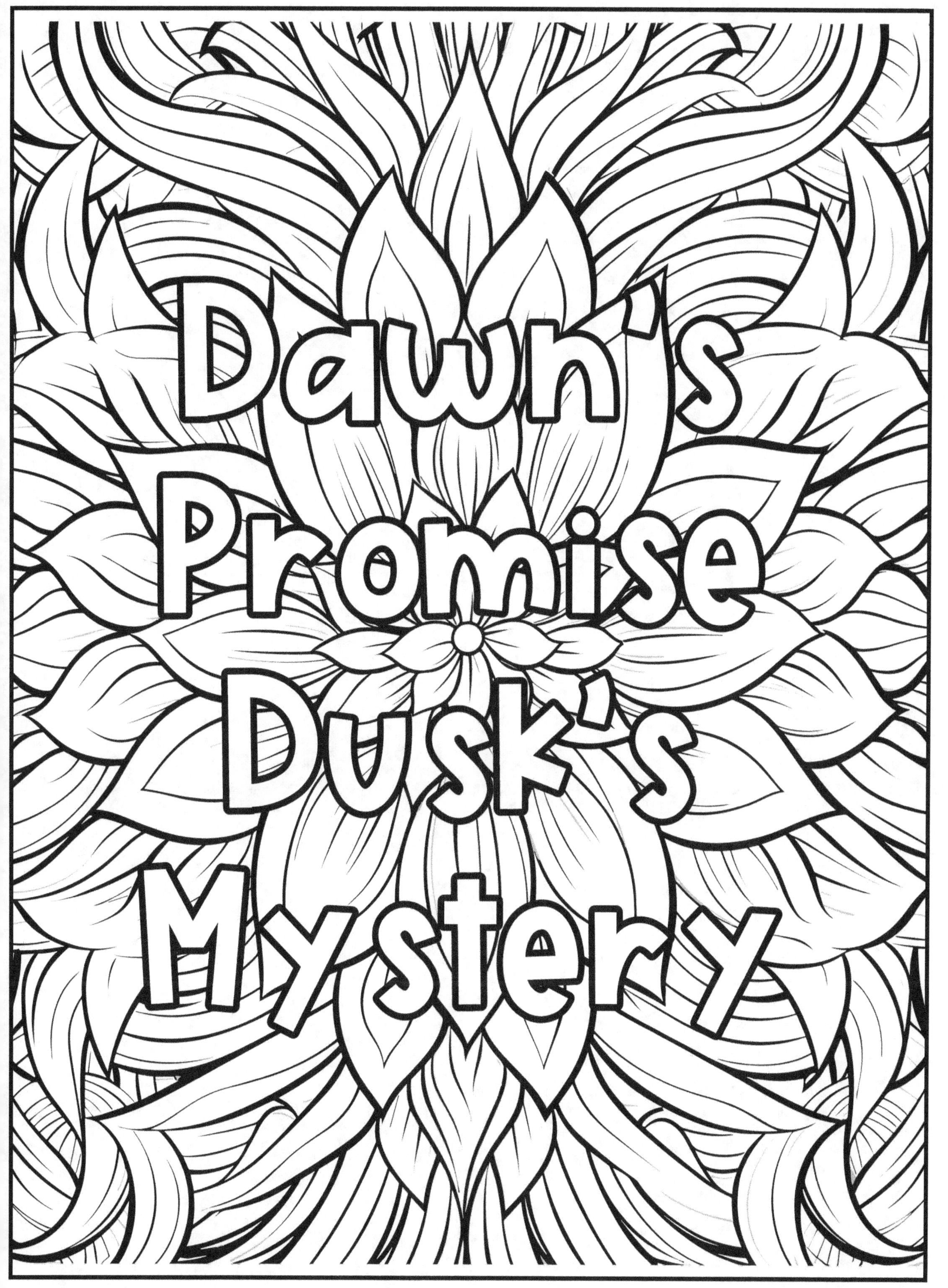

Dawn's
Promise
Dusk's
Mystery

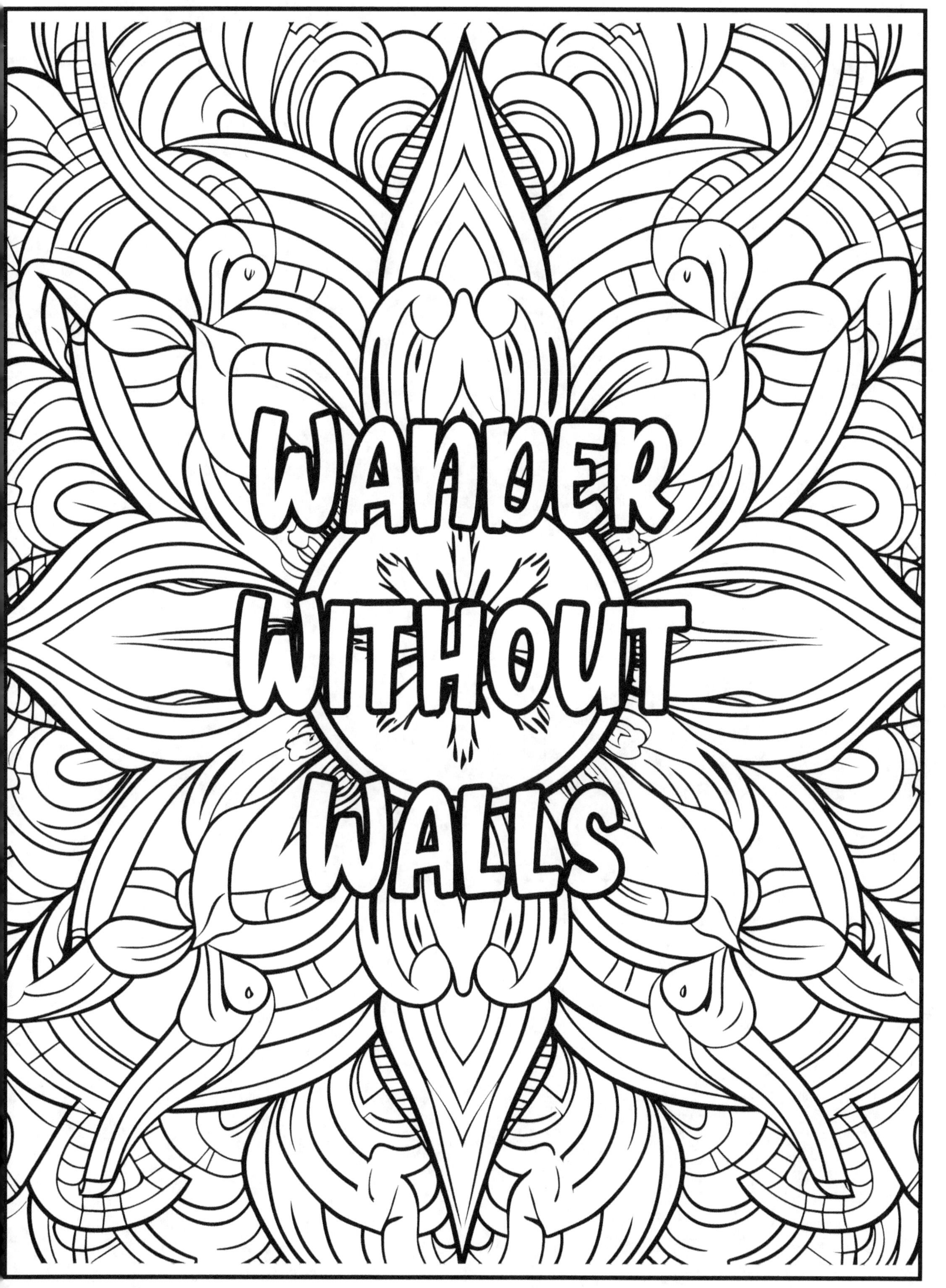

WANDER
WITHOUT
WALLS

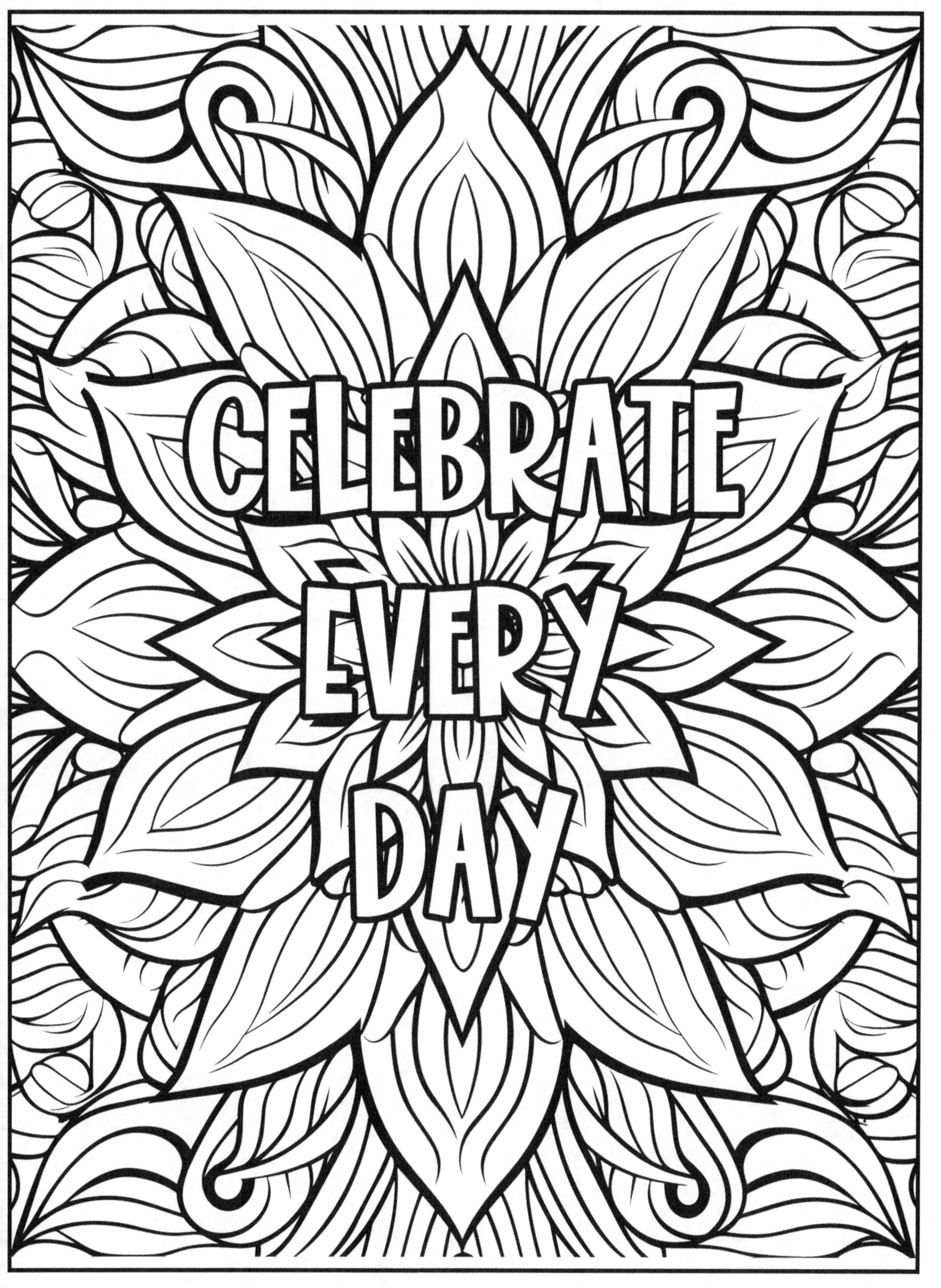

CELEBRATE
EVERY
DAY

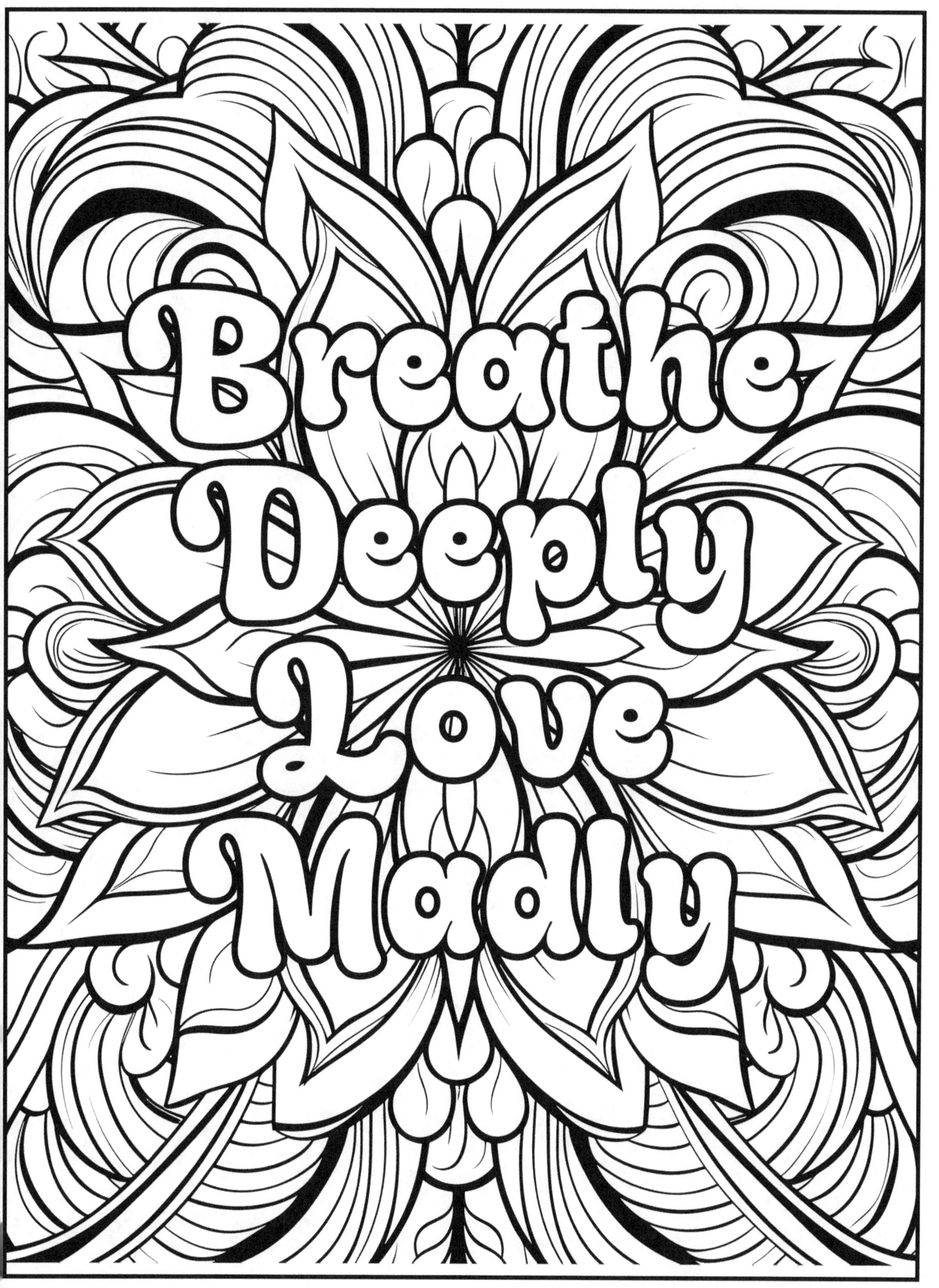

Breathe
Deeply
Love
Madly

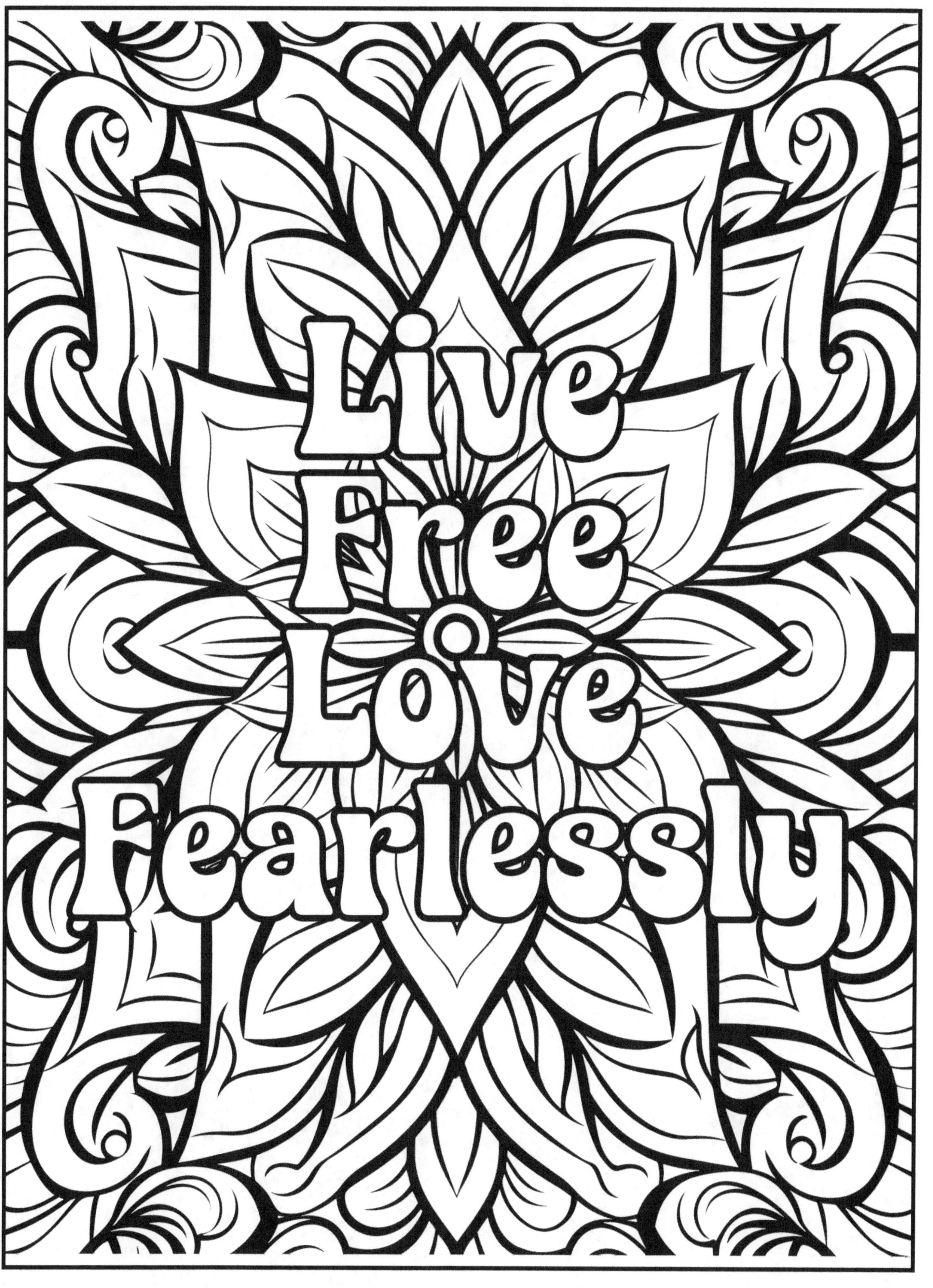

Live
Free
Love
Fearlessly

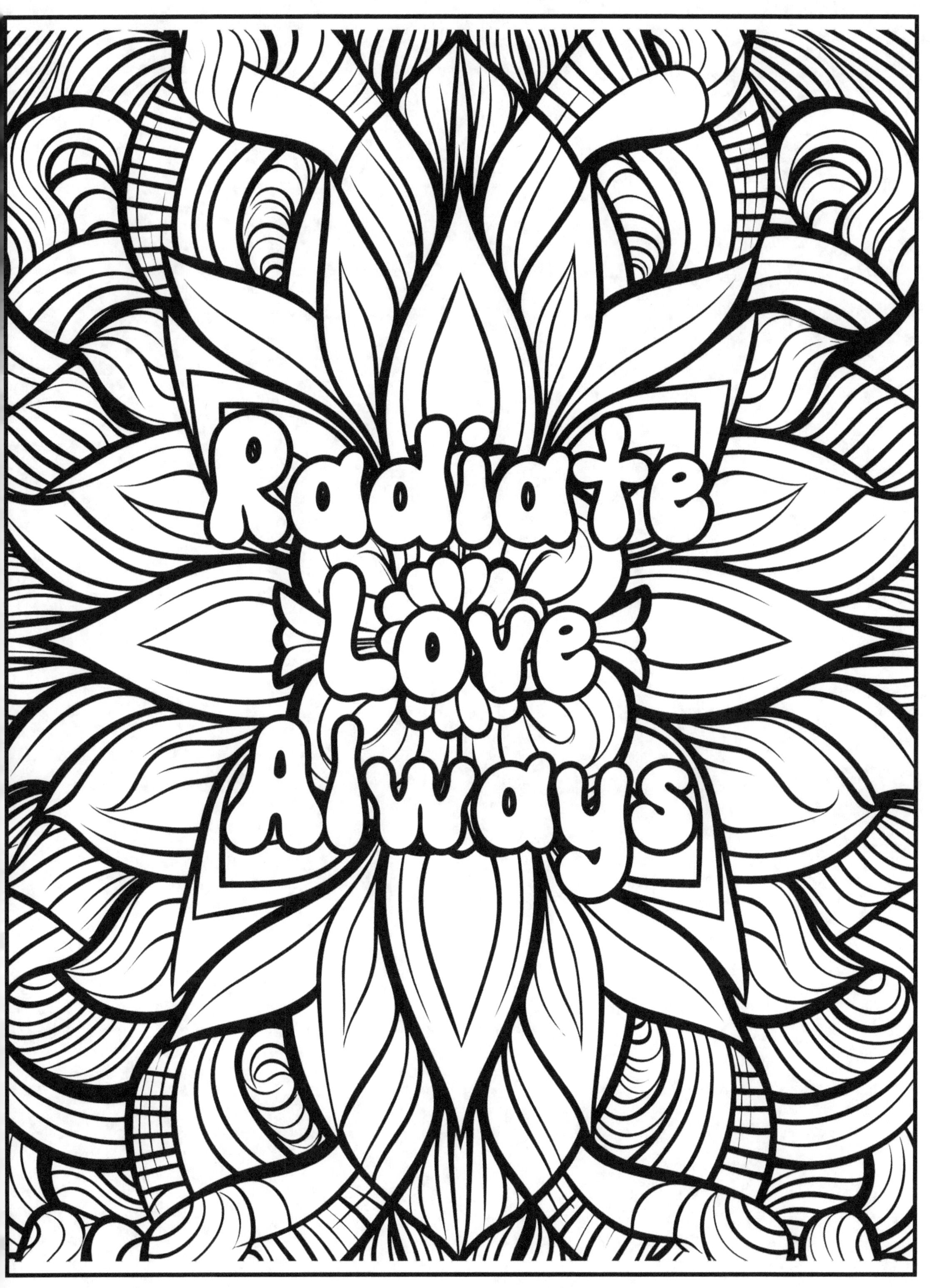
Radiate
Love
Always

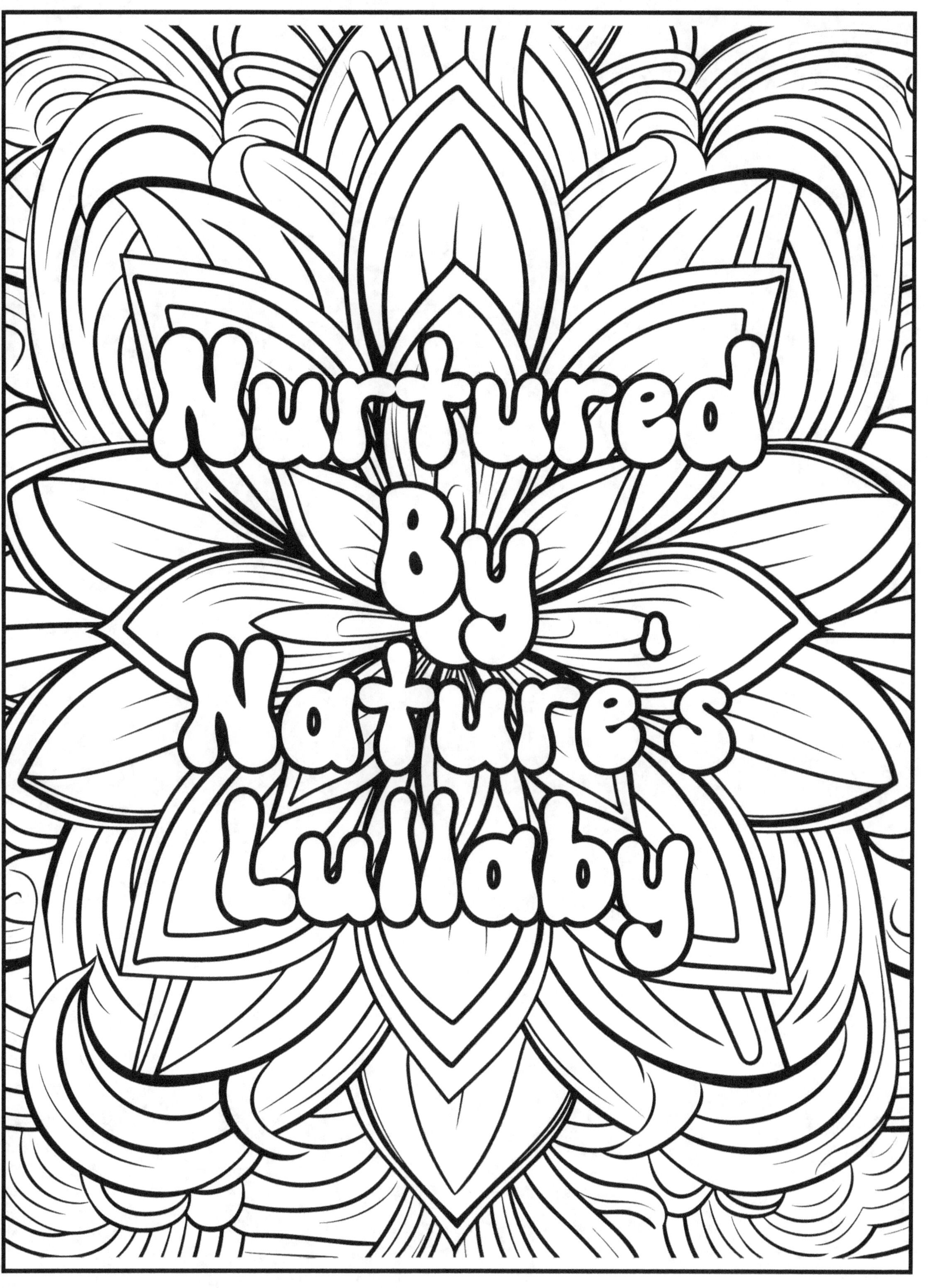

Nurtured
By
Nature's
Lullaby

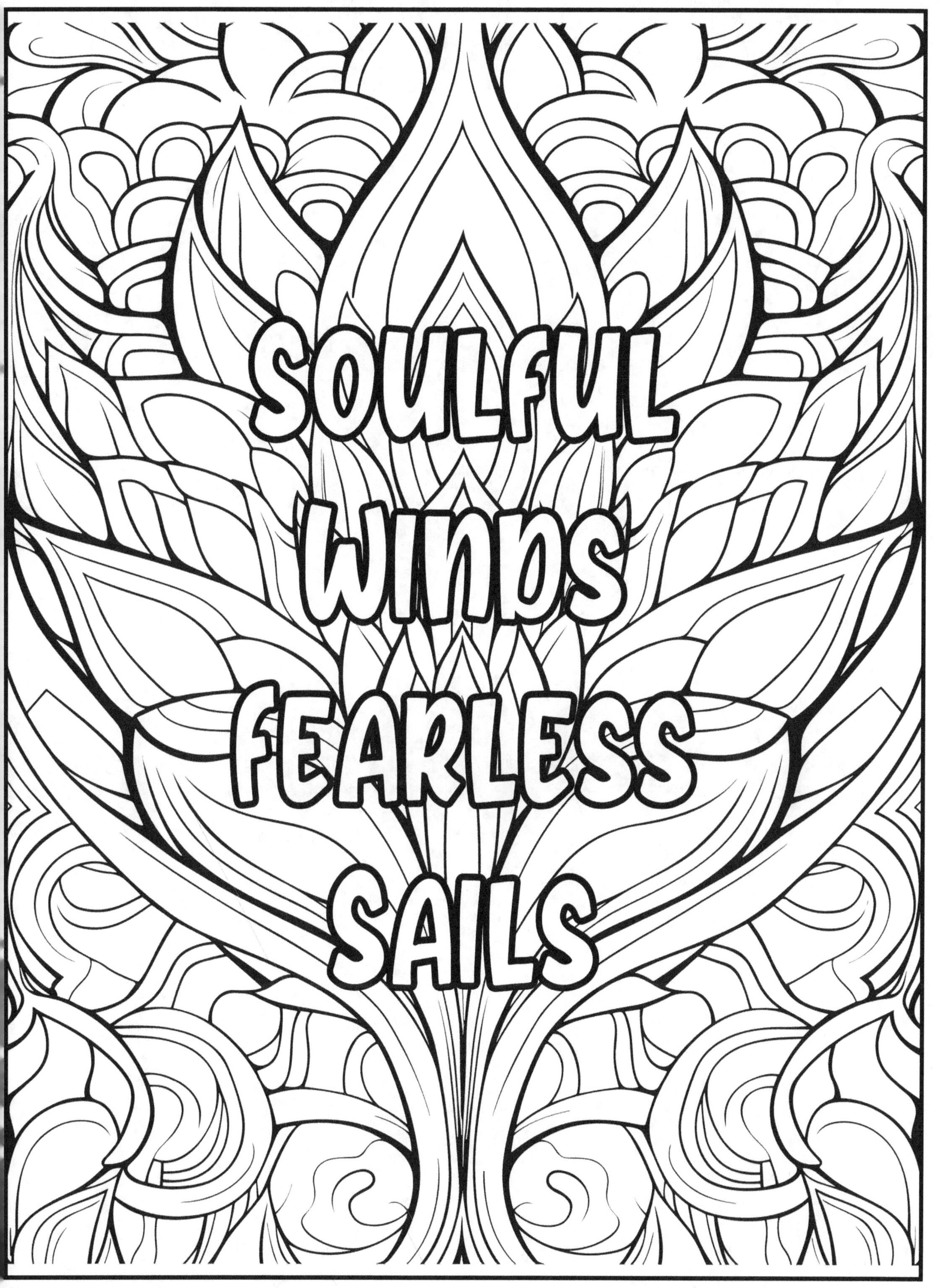

SOULFUL
WINDS
FEARLESS
SAILS

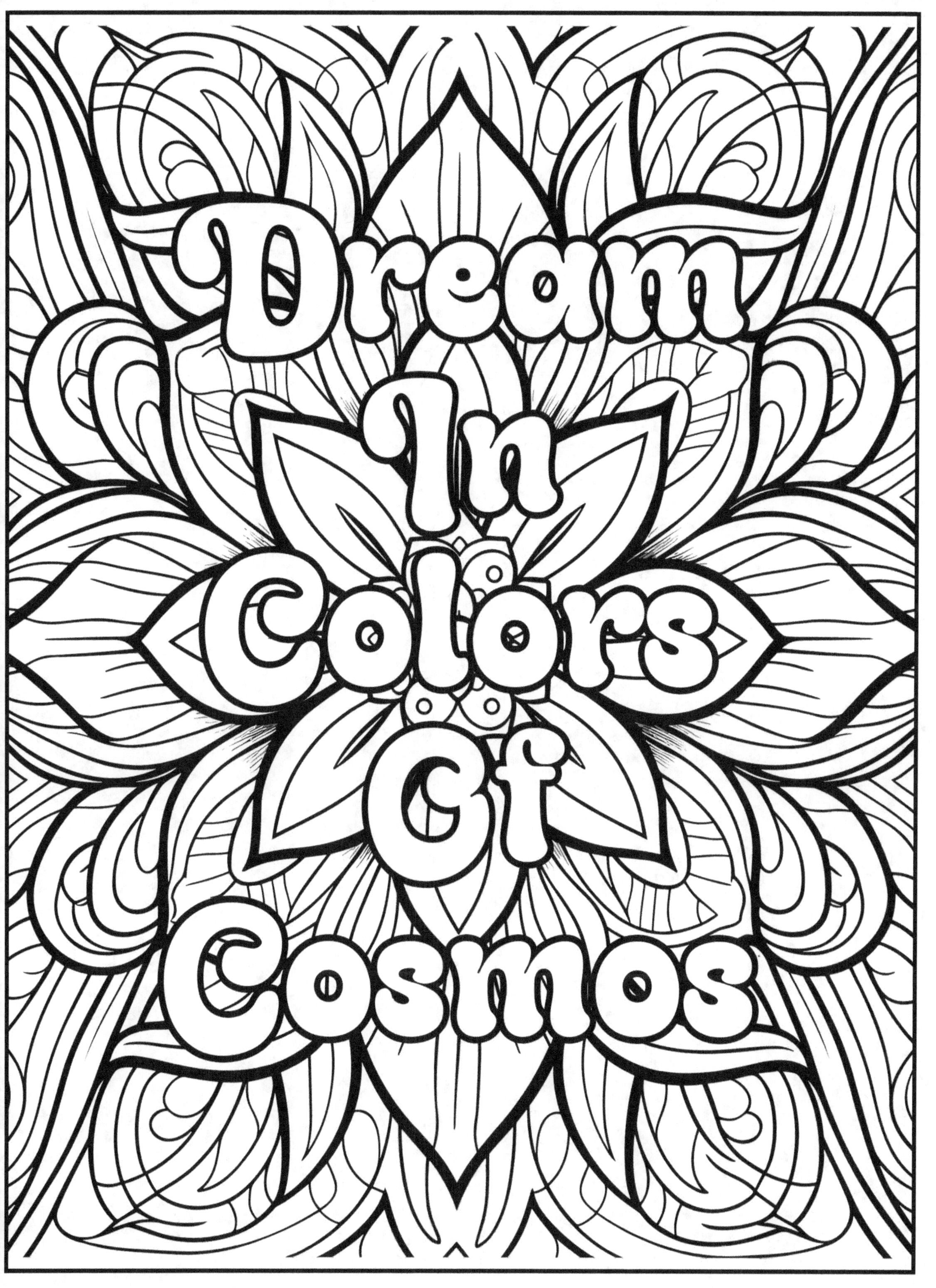

Dream In Colors Of Cosmos

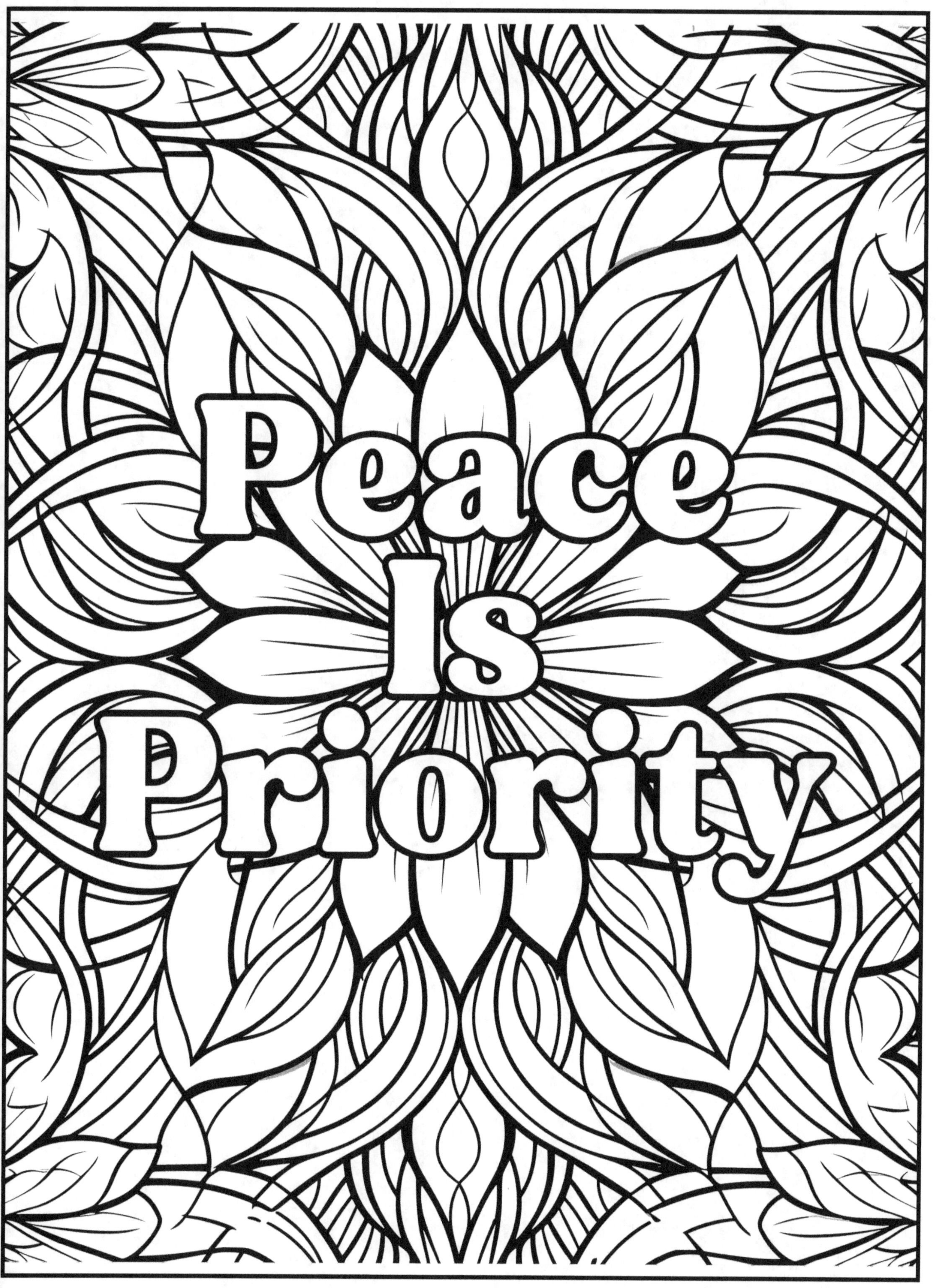

Peace
Is
Priority

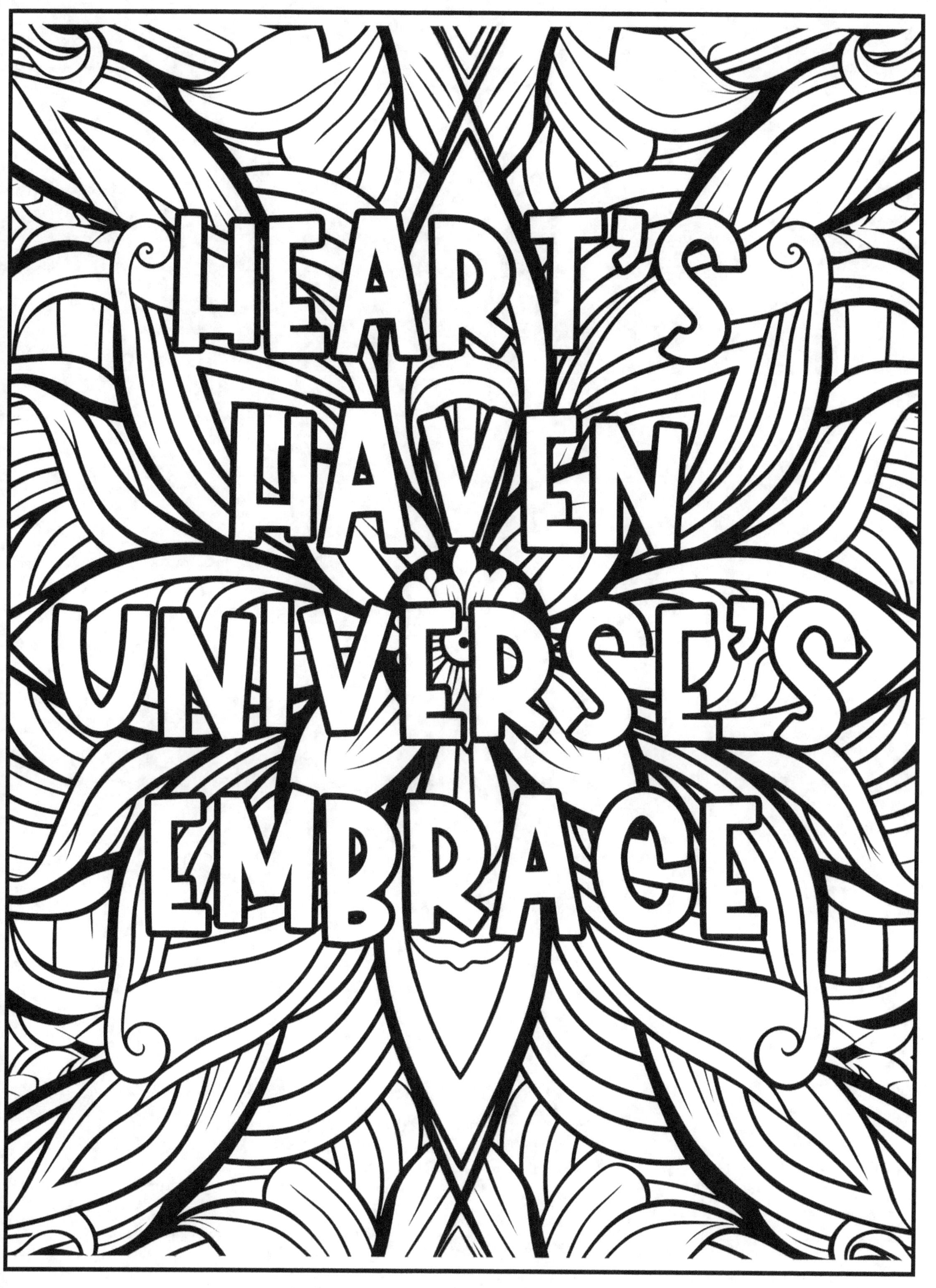
HEART'S
HAVEN
UNIVERSE'S
EMBRACE

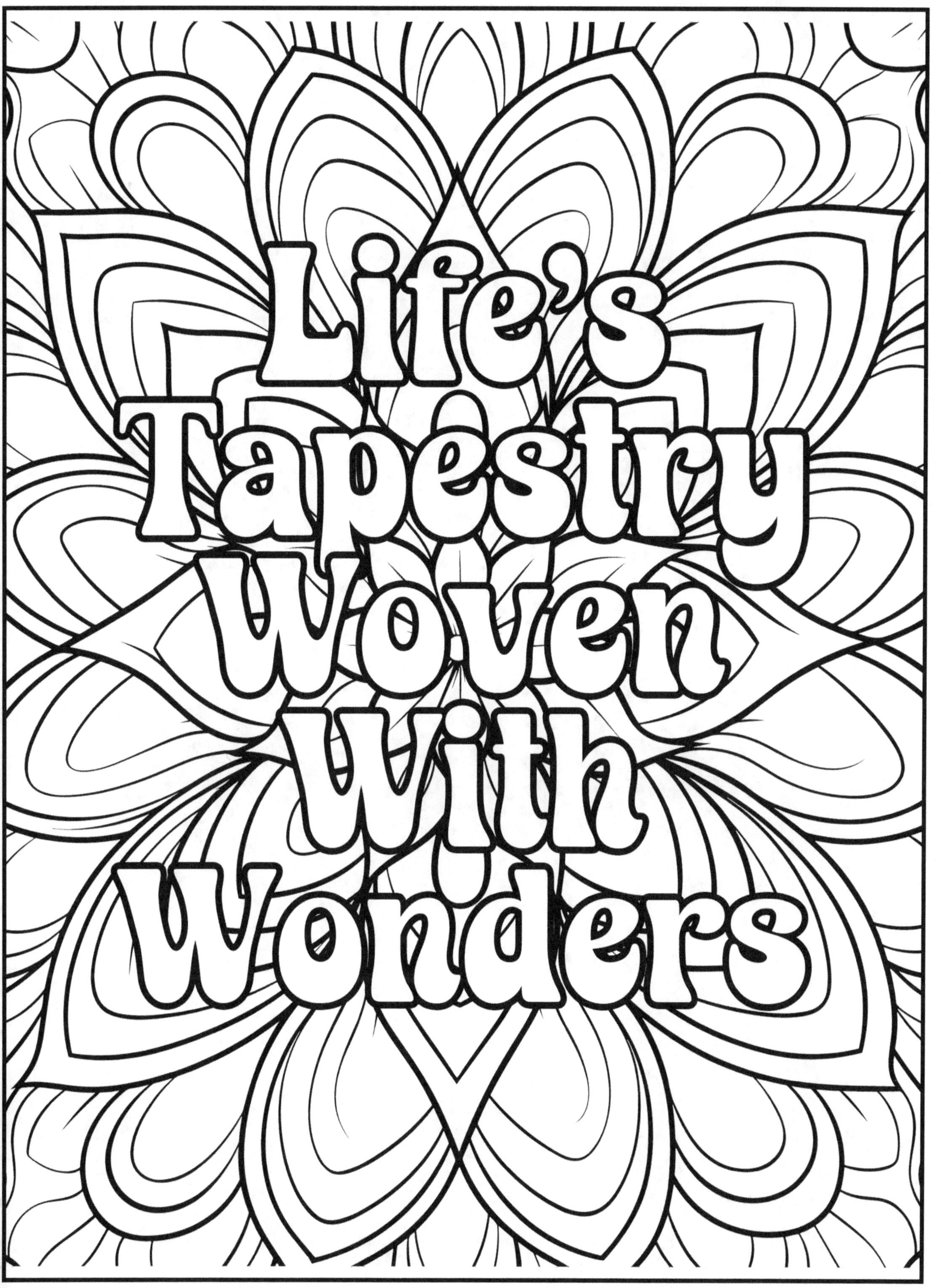
Life's
Tapestry
Woven
With
Wonders

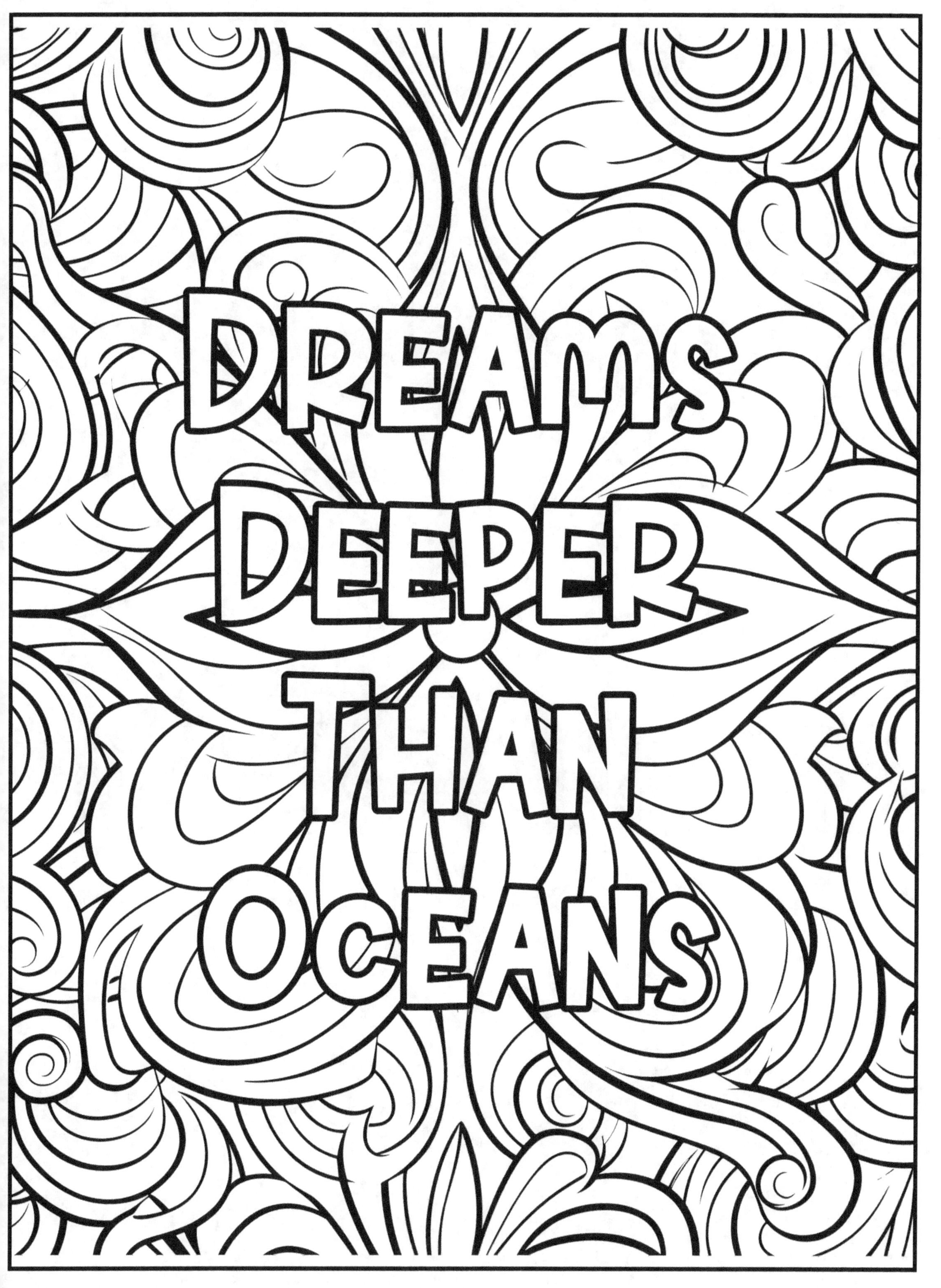
DREAMS
DEEPER
THAN
OCEANS

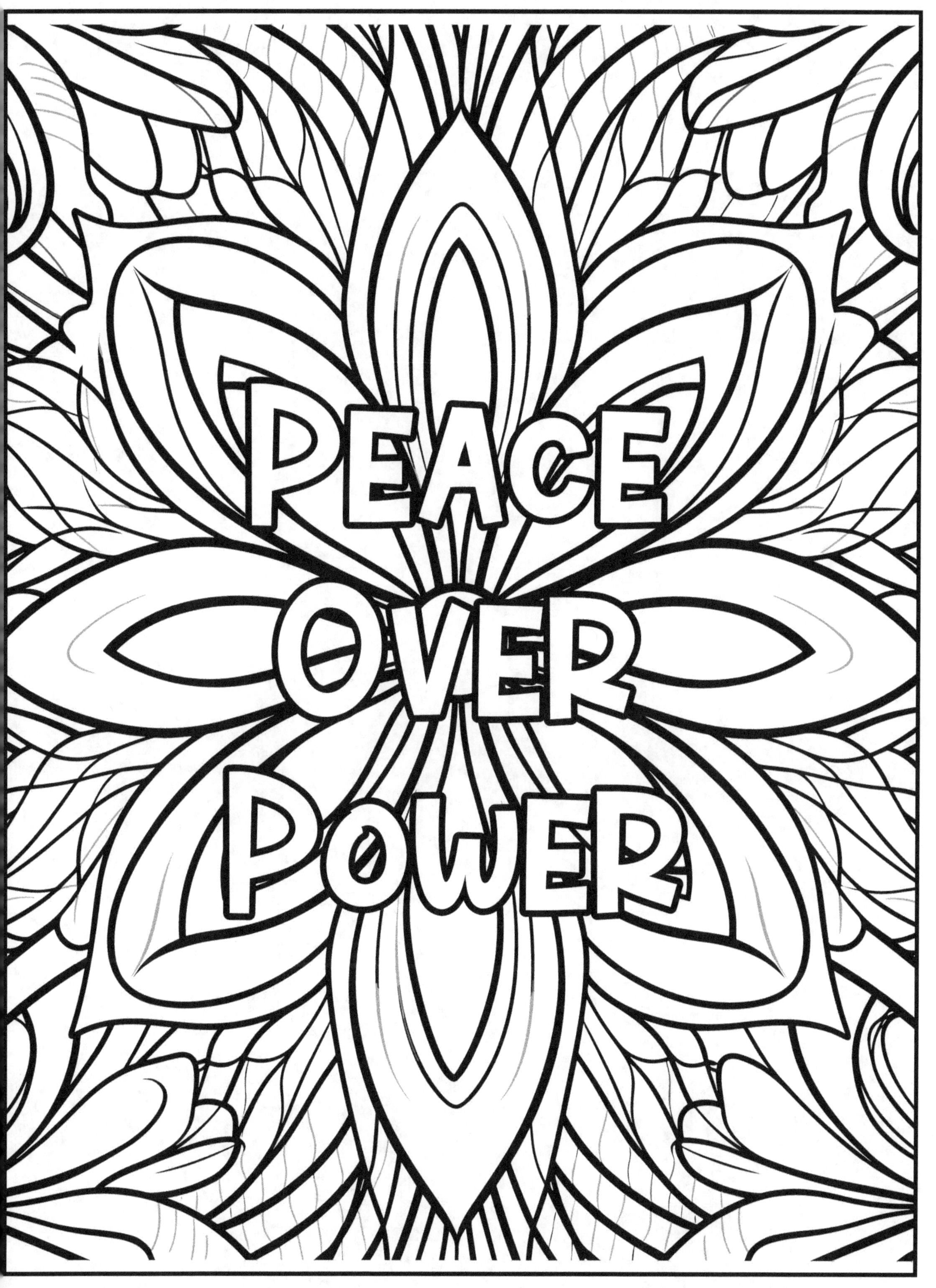

PEACE
OVER
POWER

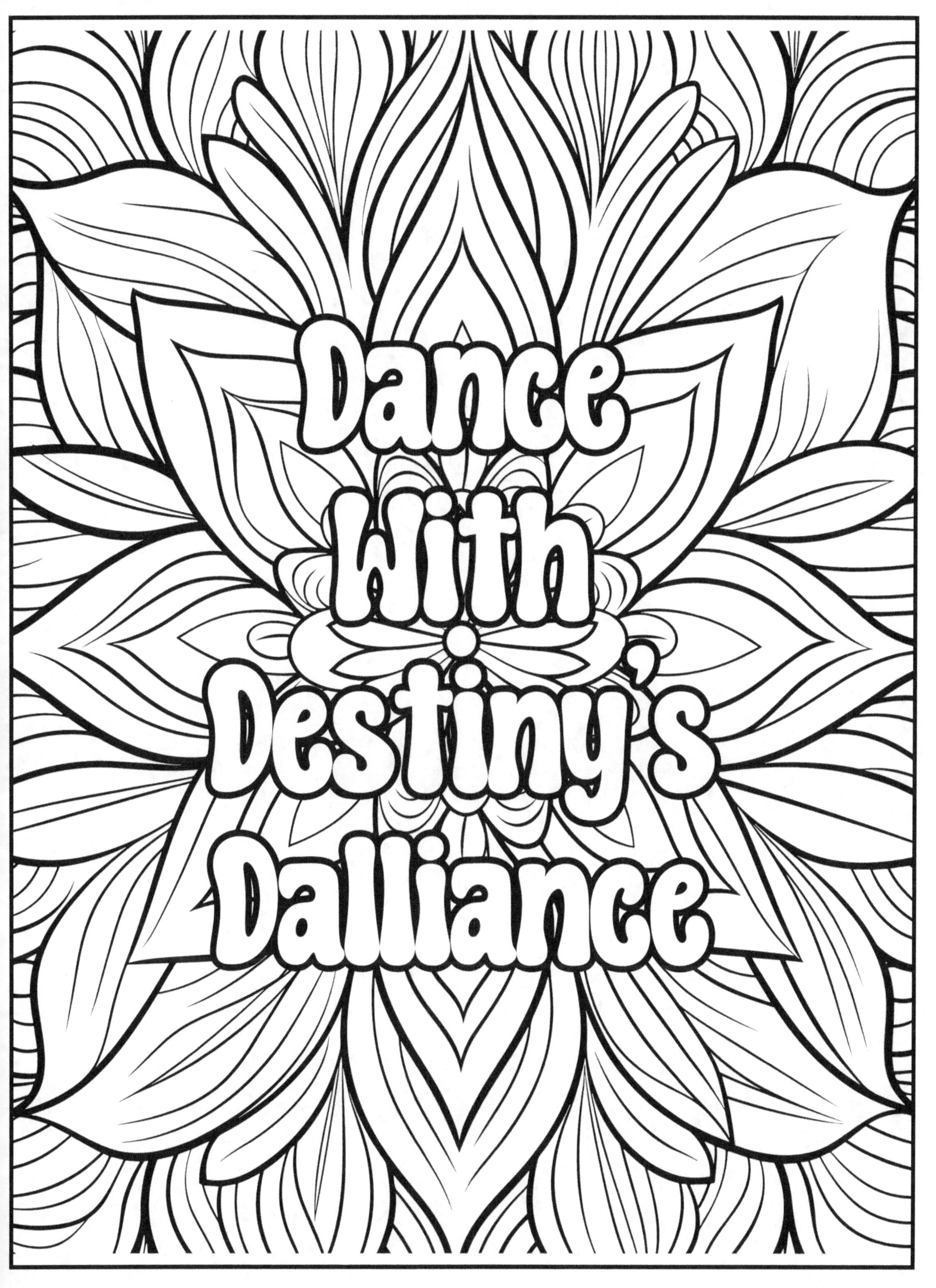

Dance
With
Destiny's
Dalliance

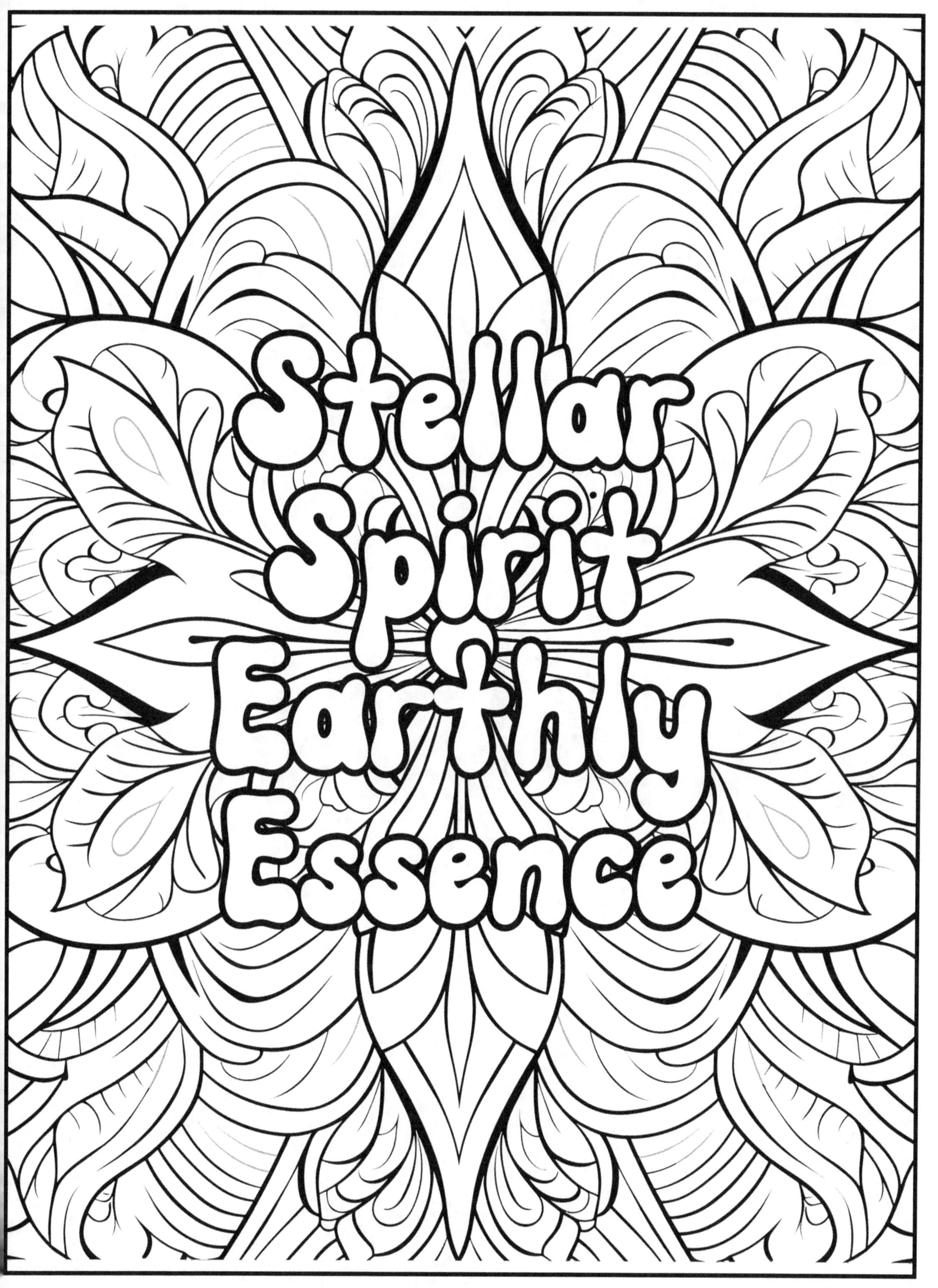

Stellar
Spirit
Earthly
Essence

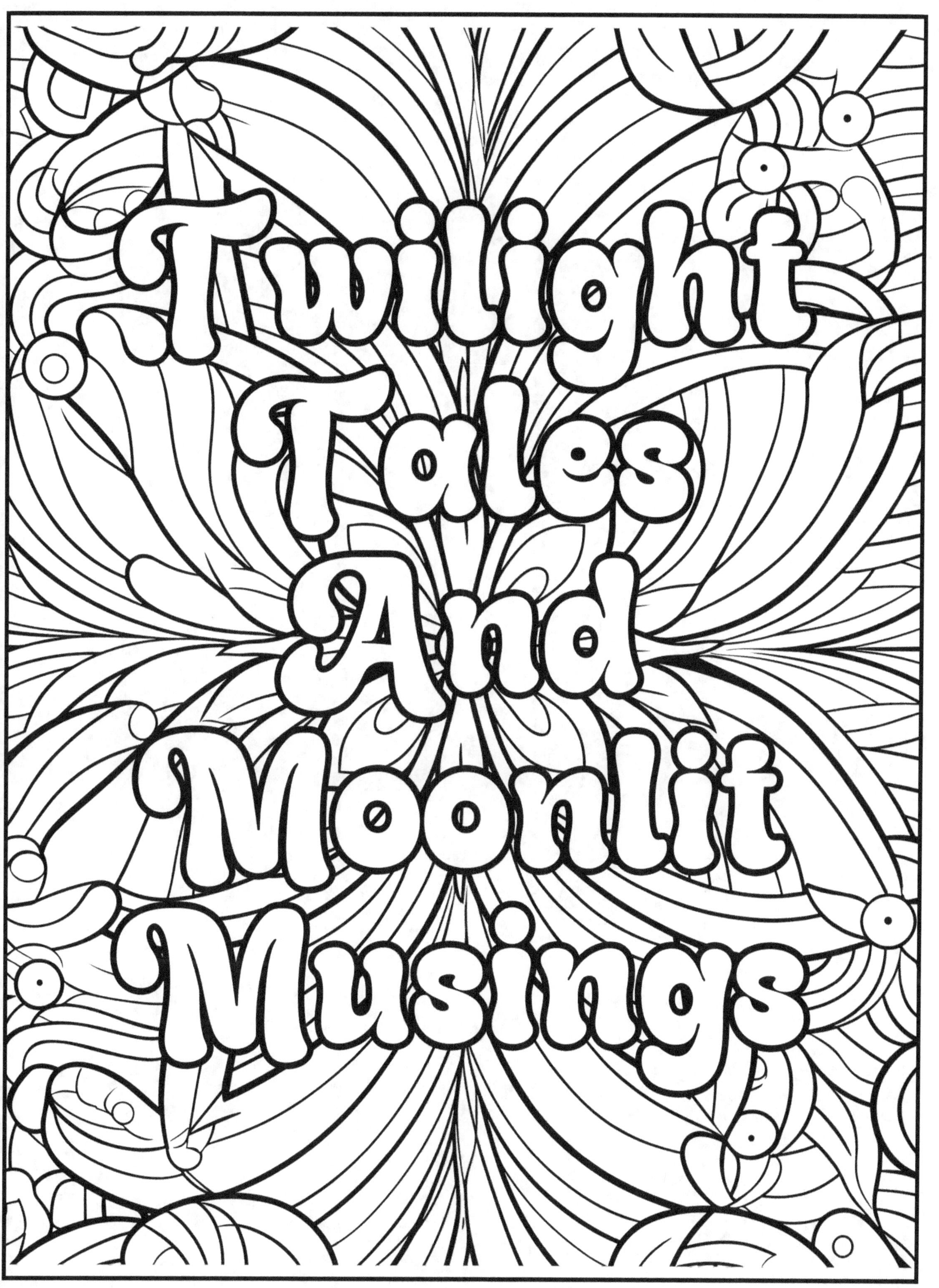

Twilight Tales And Moonlit Musings

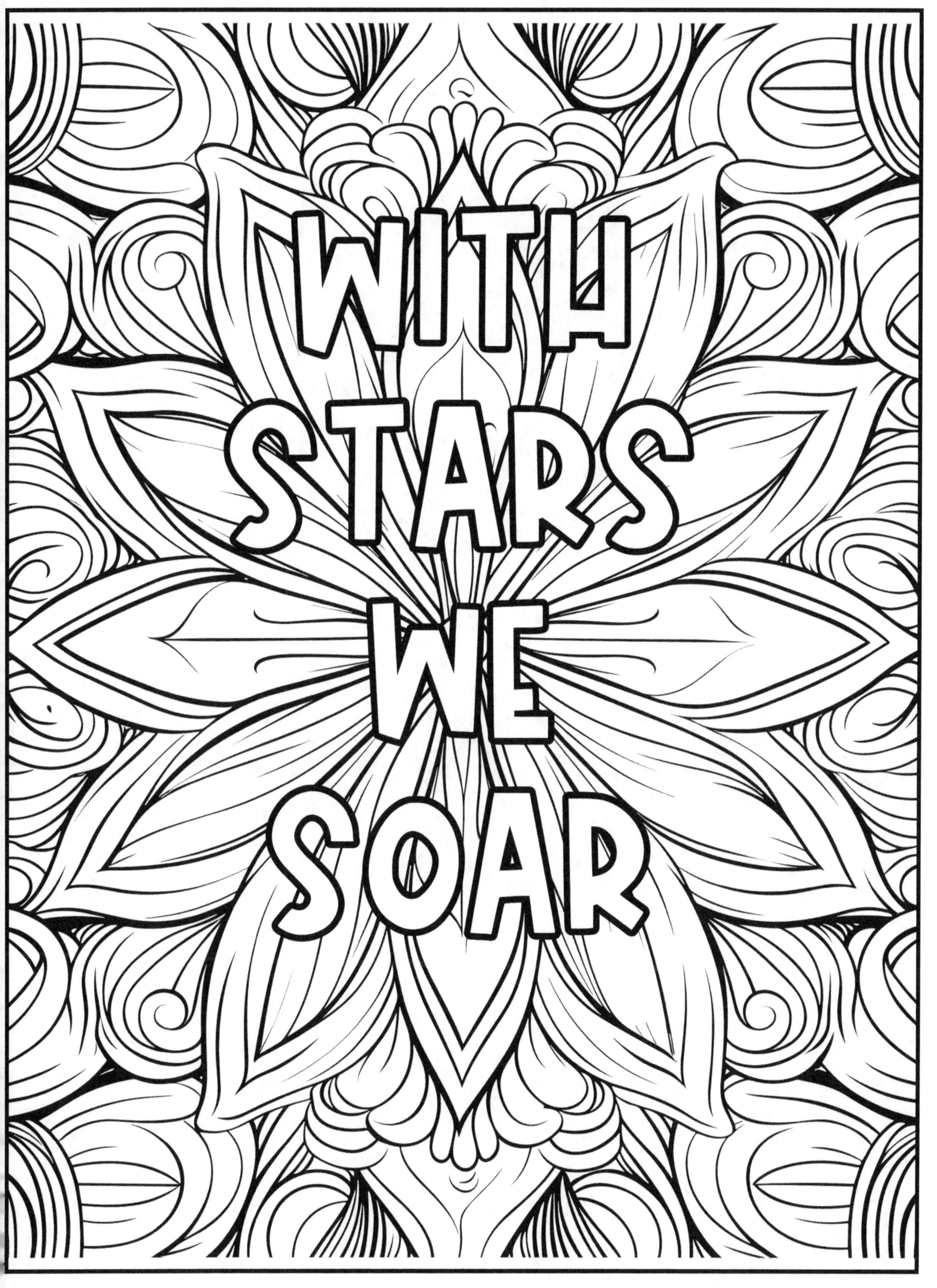

WITH
STARS
WE
SOAR

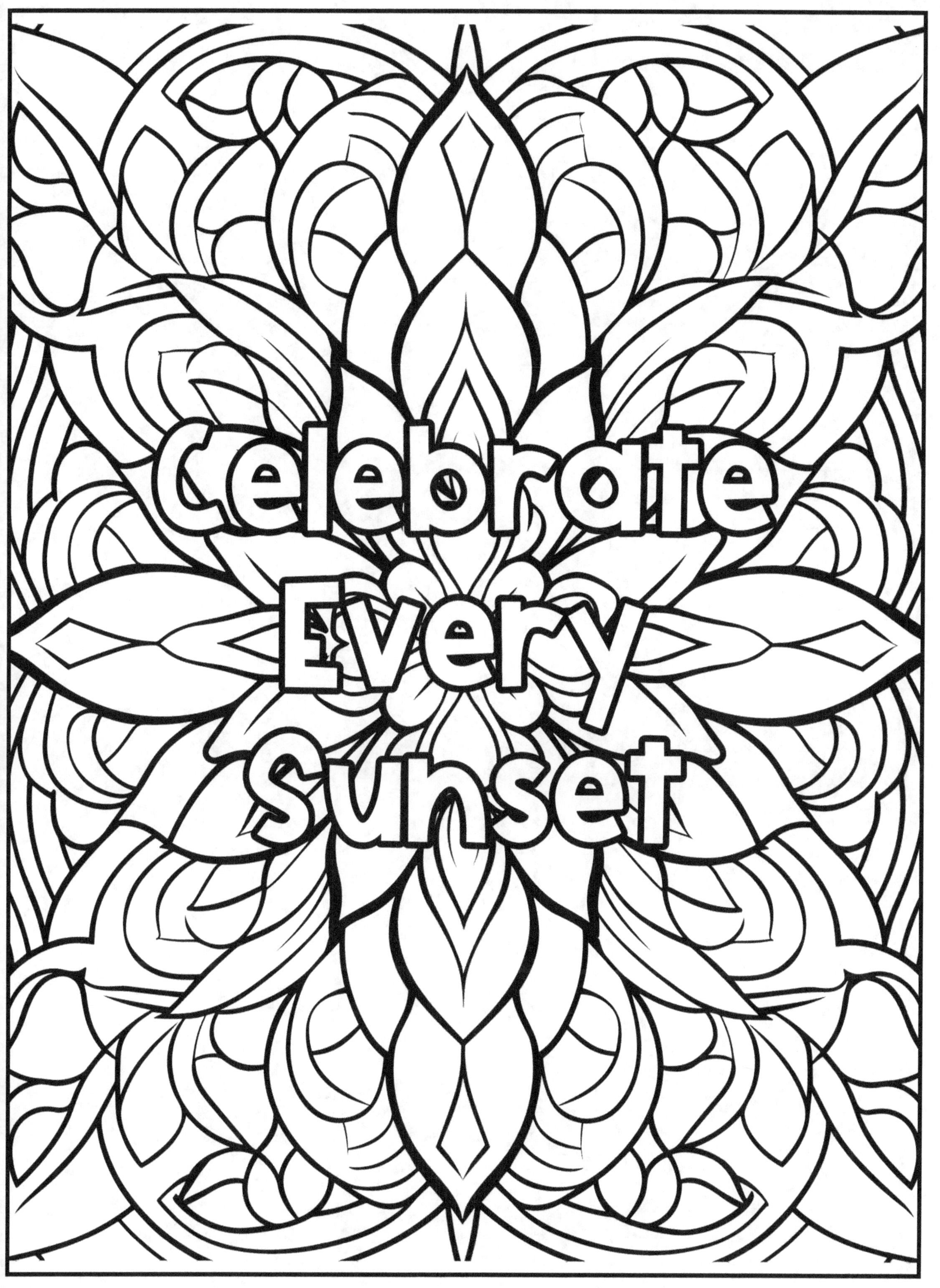

Celebrate
Every
Sunset

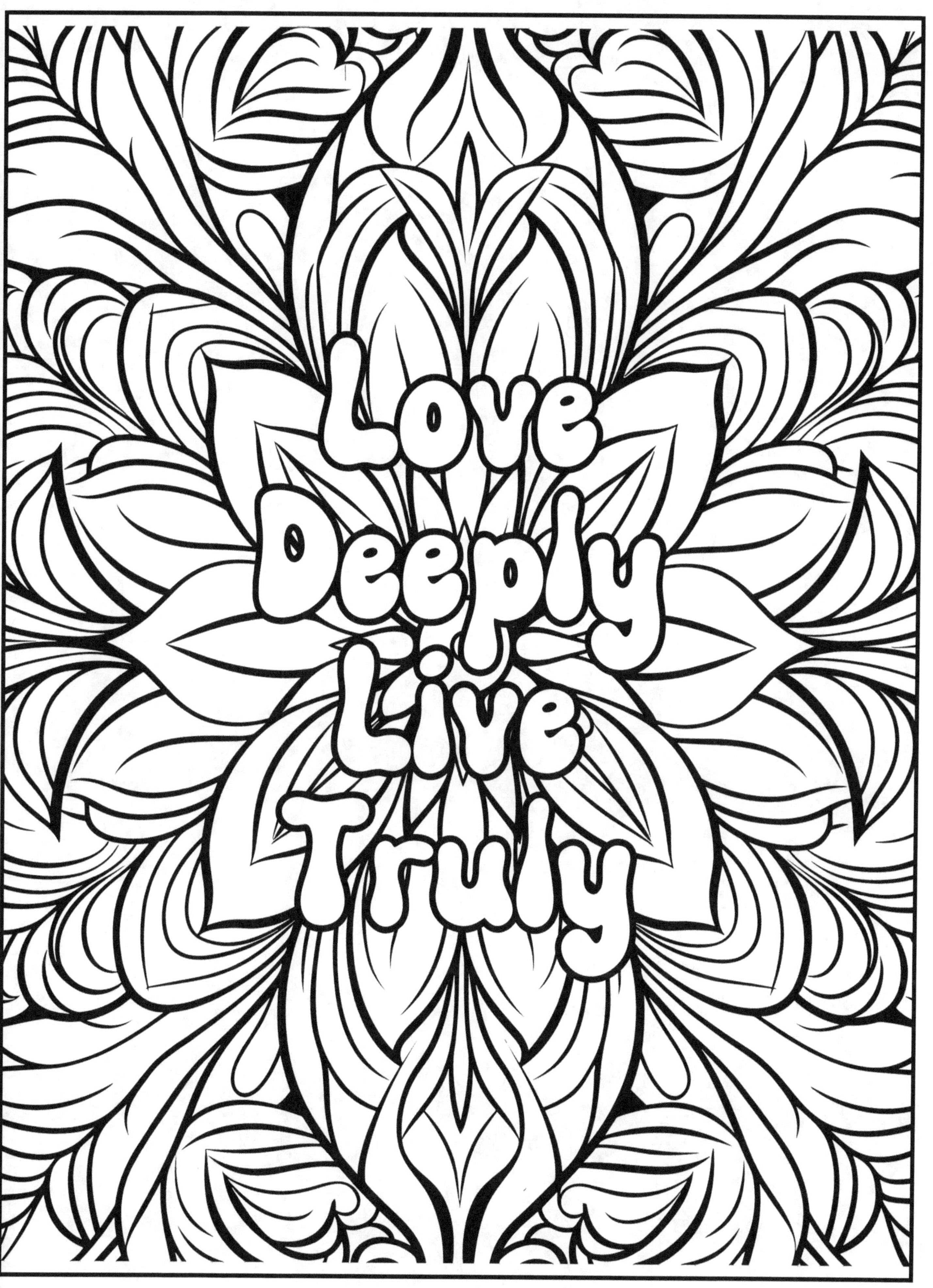

Love
Deeply
Live
Truly

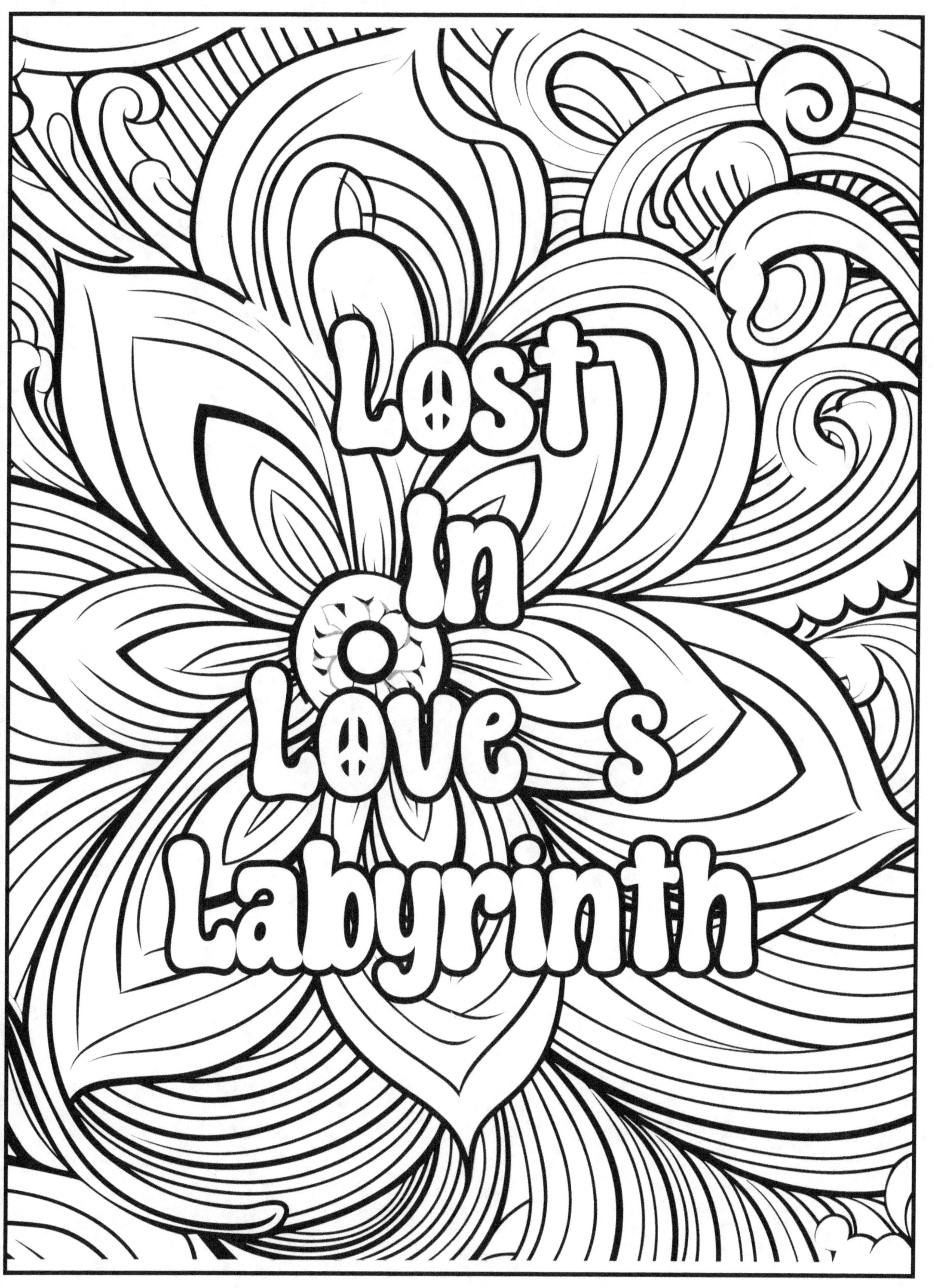

Lost
In
Love's
Labyrinth

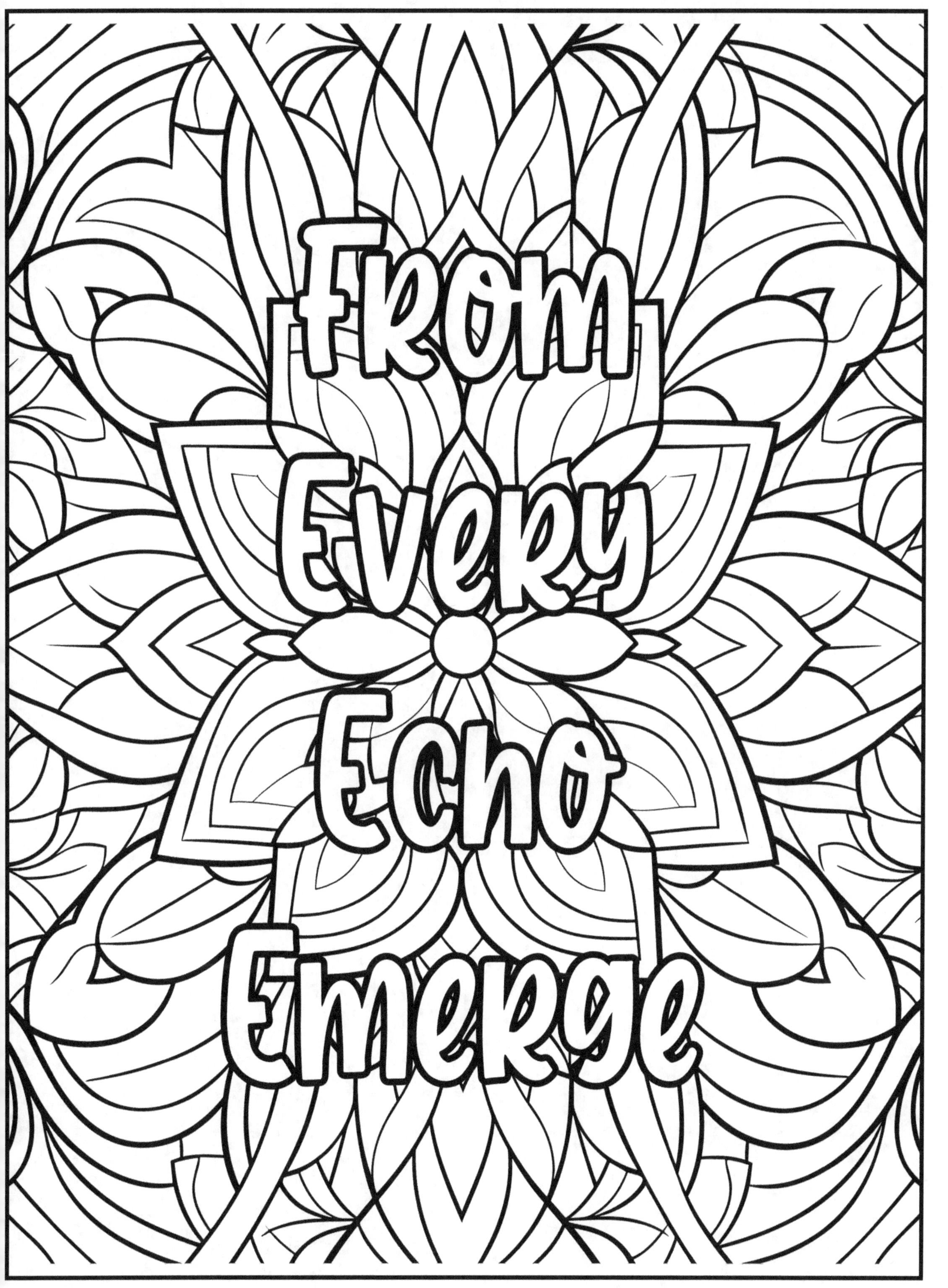

From
Every
Echo
Emerge

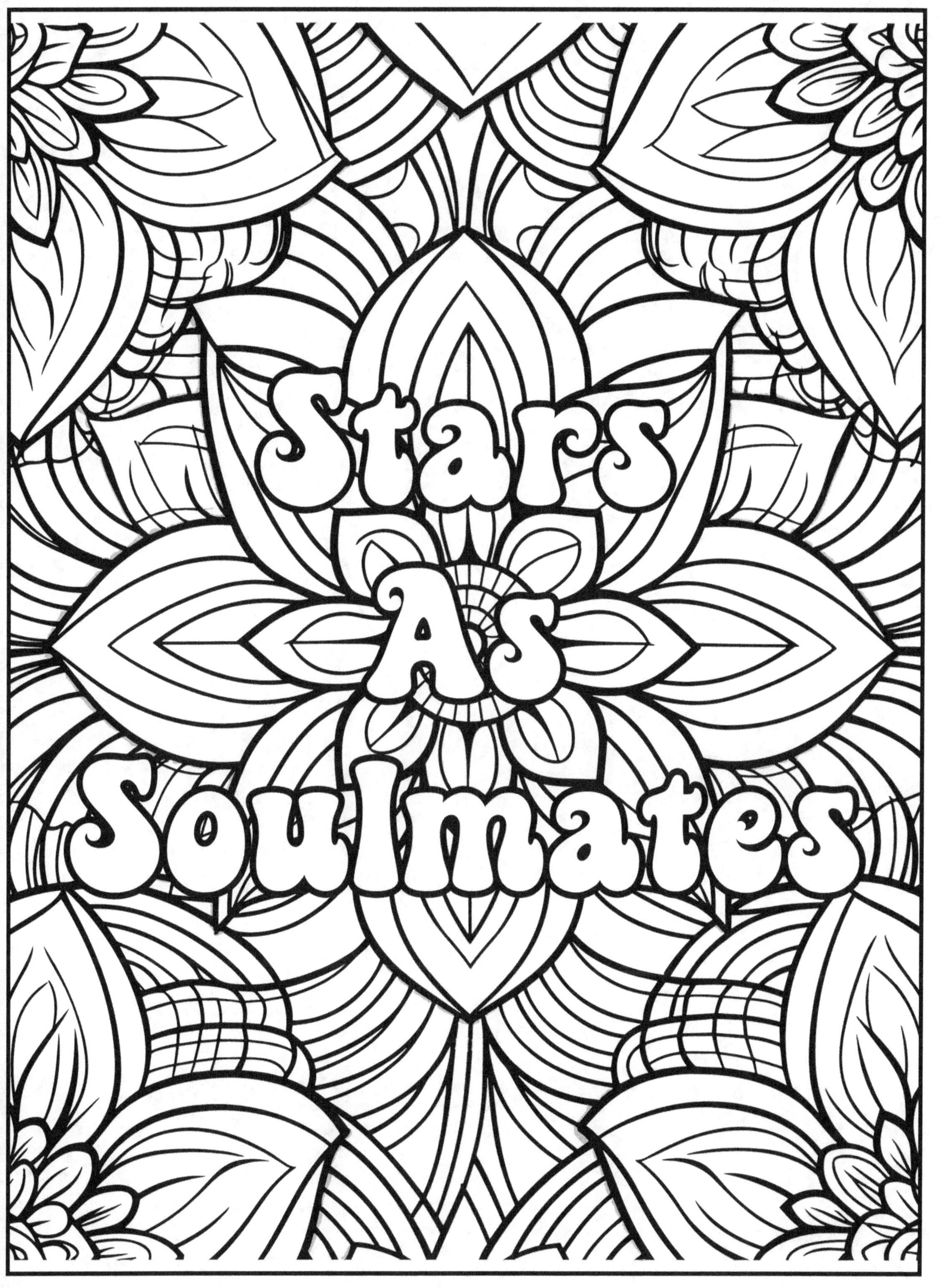
Stars
As
Soulmates

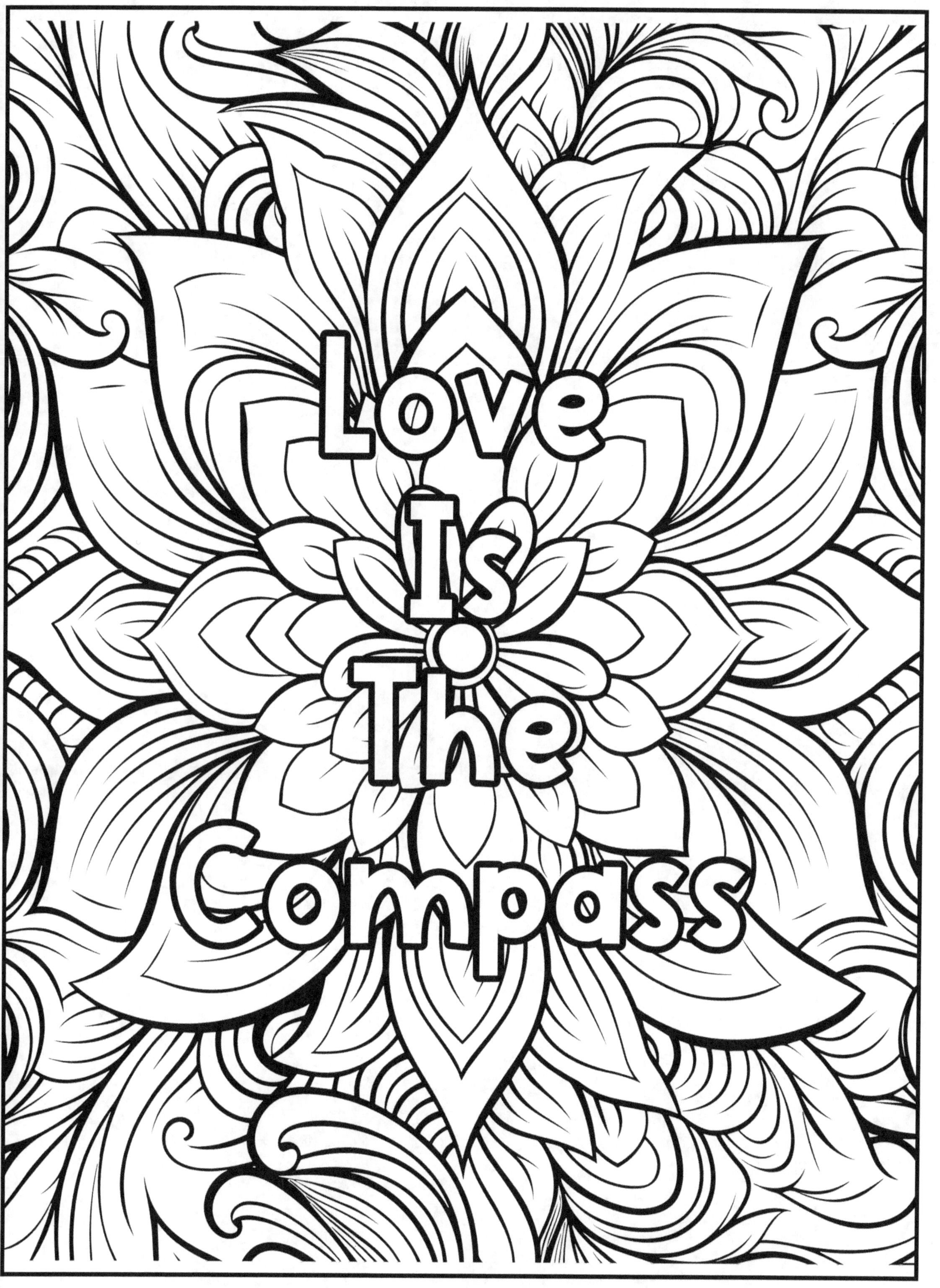
Love
Is
The
Compass

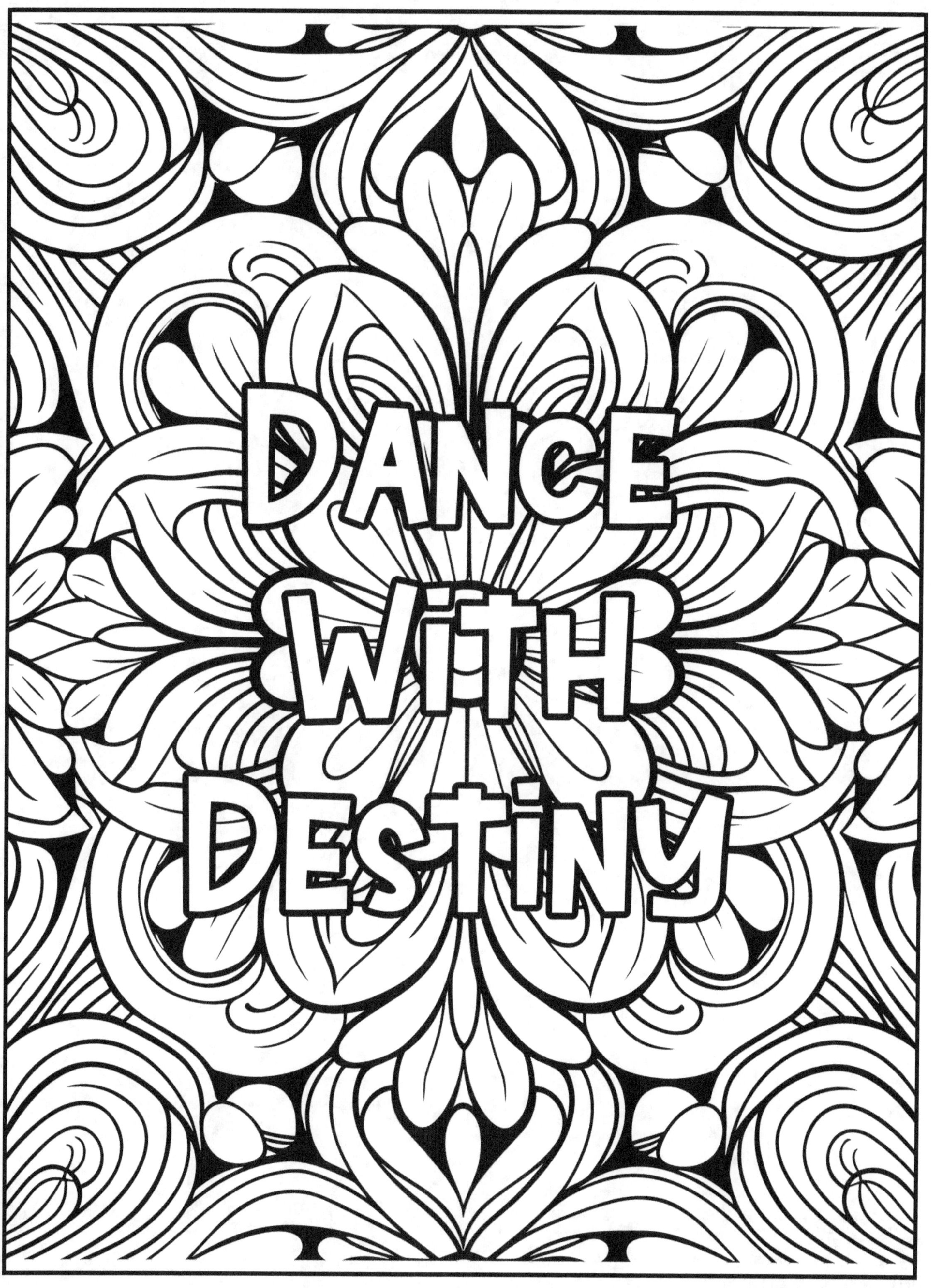

DANCE
WITH
DESTINY

www.ingramcontent.com/pod-product-compliance
Lightning Source LLC
Chambersburg PA
CBHW080939260726
48661CB00010B/3983